GETTING EXCITED ABOUT DATA

GETTING EXCITED ABOUT DATA

How to Combine People, Passion, and Proof

Edie L. Holcomb

CORWIN PRESS, INC.
A Sage Publications Company
Thousand Oaks, California

For information address:

 Corwin Press, Inc.
A Sage Publications Company
2455 Teller Road
Thousand Oaks, California 91320
E-mail: order@corwinpress.com

SAGE Publications Ltd.
6 Bonhill Street
London EC2A 4PU
United Kingdom

SAGE Publications India Pvt. Ltd.
M-32 Market
Greater Kailash I
New Delhi 110 048 India

Printed in the United States of America

Library of Congress Cataloging-in-Publication Data

Holcomb, Edie L.
    Getting excited about data: How to combine people, passion,
and proof / by Edie L. Holcomb.
      p. cm.
    Includes bibliographical references.
    ISBN 0-8039-6738-1 (cloth: acid-free paper)
    ISBN 0-8039-6739-X (pbk.: acid-free paper)
    1. Educational indicators—United States. 2. Educational
evaluation—United States. 3. Education—United States—Statistics.
4. School improvement programs—United States. 5. Academic
achievement—United States. I. Title.
    LB2846 .H56 1998
    379.1′58—ddc21   98-25462

This book is printed on acid-free paper.

99 00 01 02 03 04 05 10 9 8 7 6 5 4 3 2 1

Editorial Assistant: Kristin L. Gibson
Production Editor: Denise Santoyo
Production Assistant: Stephanie Allen
Typesetter/Designer: Janelle LeMaster
Cover Designer: Michelle Lee

Contents

List of Figures

Foreword

Data—it's such a dilemma. We know we must provide it because educators are continually challenged to prove their worth. Increased attention to privatization of schools, vouchers, and accountability dictates the need for black-and-white proof that our work in schools makes a difference. But what data and how much do we collect? How do we analyze it and report it? What do we do with the findings that will improve the next round of results? How do we ensure that "what gets measured gets done"? And how do we sustain people's passion for teaching and learning while devoting time and energy to the more pedantic tasks of generating proof?

Getting Excited About Data: How to Combine People, Passion, and Proof answers these questions. The book outlines a process for producing concrete evidence. It stresses the importance of enlisting broad stakeholder involvement. It focuses attention on strategically aligning all elements of the organization around the essential mission of maximizing student success. By analyzing what is and is not working to improve student learning, educators can focus scarce resources on goals and strategies that make the most impact on achievement. Time is the most critical resource, and this book can help schools use time more effectively. The time invested in "data work" can generate a net savings if it guides the school toward decisions that pay dividends in student achievement.

A visit to any library or college bookstore will reveal many volumes about data, statistics, and improving education. But something must be missing. In all our work with Kentucky education reform, through the Effective Schools projects and now through consolidated planning for the Improving America's Schools Act, the most problematic aspects have been use of data in needs assessment and use of data to document improvement.

Edie Holcomb's first book, *Asking the Right Questions: Tools and Techniques for Teamwork* was a major contribution. The popularity of that text, now in its fourth printing and one of Corwin's convention best-sellers, illustrates how educators are starved for information that is well organized, easy to read, engaging, and practical. It addressed the use of data enough to whet our appetites, and many readers like me begged for more.

Getting Excited About Data is Holcomb's response. This is not another statistics book that focuses on theoretical information, but a very practical "how to" manual. It is written to the level of readiness in most schools, establishing a common knowledge base and moving to the next level of application in real-life settings. Certainly, a book about data must include graphs and statistics, but therein lies the difference between this book and others. *Getting Excited About Data* is not "antistatistics"; it is authentic *application* of statistics as they can be really used in schools. Only someone who thoroughly comprehends both statistical processes and the realities of interactions in schools could convey such complex content with the simplicity and practicality of this author.

Getting Excited About Data sets the stage for improving schools by providing school leaders, parents, and constituents with practical knowledge about how to focus on what schools are about—student learning. It provides tools educators desperately need and accompanies them with strategies and helpful hints for usage. Engaging stories make the reading entertaining as well as informative.

Following this step-by-step approach will establish a paradigm of shared leadership, collaboration, and communication. Increasing organizational capacity and using staff time in the most productive manner will be by-products. An old adage states, "In God we trust; all others use data." This book shows educators how to use data in a manner that establishes our trustworthiness.

—Deborah H. McDonald

Kentucky Distinguished Educator
Consolidated Planning Coordinator
Division of School Improvement
Kentucky Department of Education

Preface

It doesn't seem so very long ago—except when I get things in the mail like invitations to 25-year reunions. But there are days when it seems like light-years. I'm referring to the "good old days" when I was a classroom teacher and my *opinion* counted. I could answer parents—or even principals—with a *subjective* statement in a sincere, confident voice, and I would be believed. Not so these days. It seems as if Missouri has taken over the union with everyone crying, "Show me." Professional judgment isn't enough; people want proof. In short, they want to see the data. But if we really think about it and learn to respond appropriately, these might just be the "good *new* days" or the "good *news* days."

Getting Excited About Data: How to Combine People, Passion, and Proof is written for all the teachers, school administrators, staff developers, and advocates of public education who want to be proactive and responsive to the communities they serve—but don't know where to start or how to start and may even be afraid to start. The book is exactly and only that—a starting point. It targets the level of readiness I've observed working with schools in more than 30 states and several countries. The adage, "Walk before you run," is taken very literally. So there are a number of things this book is *not*.

This Is Not a Statistics Book. The uses of data recommended in this book require the ability to count, calculate averages and percentages, and construct simple graphs. Regression formulas and correlation coefficients are omitted. Here the term *significance* isn't represented as $p < .05$. It refers instead to what the *school* defines as significant, that is, important, relevant, and useful to know.

This Is Not a Technical Manual. *Getting Excited About Data* was not written to develop technical expertise. Its focus is on the human element—hopes and fears, prior knowledge, and current needs. It offers a variety of staff development activities to create active engagement with data and interaction with peers that will build more collaborative cultures with a sense of collective responsibility for student learning.

This Book Is Not Bureaucratic and Impersonal. This book won't turn anyone into an accountant or auditor or undertaker. Its purpose is to affirm and build on the nurturing nature of teachers, adding the support of objective information to their usually accurate professional intuition. Stories such as the one in Chapter 9 illustrate how the use of data can stimulate greater sensitivity to the needs of students, not "turn them into numbers."

This Book Is Not Comprehensive. If psychometricians describe this book as simplistic and basic, we will know we've been successful. There are legitimate reasons why most educators are uncomfortable with the use of data. The purpose of this book is to raise comfort and interest levels so readers will become "ready, willing, and able" to explore more sophisticated uses of data. My intent is simply this: to meet people where they are and help them take their next developmental step in a new skill area.

This Book Is Not Written in Jargon. For this book, I have intentionally chosen a casual, conversational style. My purpose is to use plain English to describe simple things I've done with real people that have created interest and opened doors. Since these activities have helped my colleagues and clients, I hope you will find them useful also.

I'm aware that the pronouns "I" and "we" are frequently interchanged throughout the book. I have let this inconsistency stand because it feels natural, because none of these activities could have occurred without the cooperation of others, and because I hope you will read as an active participant in mental dialogue with me.

This Book Is Not Aimed at Individual Student Diagnosis. The scope of *Getting Excited About Data: How to Combine People, Passion, and Proof* is the school and the district, not the individual student. For example, test scores are used in this book for organizational purposes such as school improvement and program evaluation. Assessment issues that relate to diagnosis of individual student performance and design of assessment instruments are purposely excluded.

What This Book *Is*

The content of *Getting Excited About Data: How to Combine People, Passion, and Proof* is organized into three major sections with unique purposes. The first three chapters serve as the knowledge base and foundation for the rest of the book. Chapter 1 is the "what we should be doing" chapter. It introduces a visual organizer that illustrates the relationships between components of school improvement and highlights the points where data are critical to align and maintain the process. Chapter 2 tells "why we should." It addresses the need to be more results oriented in educational planning and suggests ways to build interest and motivation for greater use of data. Chapter 3 describes the limited ways in which data are used in most school districts and explains "why we don't."

The next seven chapters are organized to reflect the components of change that are described in Chapter 1 and answer the "how to" questions. The "passion" part of the subtitle is aroused in Chapter 4, which begins with a process to engage the school's staff in revisiting the core values of the school and looking for evidence that the mission is being accomplished. Chapter 5 introduces five key questions that help determine the types of "proof" that will be meaningful and stimulate curiosity and action. Chapter 6 describes characteristics of user-friendly data, with helpful tips and examples of data displays. The importance of having "people" engage collectively in interpretation of data about their school is stressed in Chapter 7, and a professional development activity for this purpose is provided. Chapter 8 describes a group process for setting goals that are data based, grounded in the school's values, and feasible. Chapter 9 describes several methods for engaging groups in further analysis of data related to areas that need improvement. Important issues about planning, implementation, and monitoring progress are discussed in Chapter 10.

The last four chapters are the "where it all fits" section. Whereas the first 10 chapters focused on work at the school level, this section adopts a K-12 district perspective. Chapter 11 describes the design of a district "Data Day" that can be used to create awareness, energy, and commitment to a more results-oriented approach. Chapter 12 points out some important issues and helpful tips for communicating about data. Chapter 13 describes how data is used as the linchpin between vertical K-12 work on curriculum and assessment and site-based work to improve teaching and the learning environment. The last chapter emphasizes the need to sustain focus and momentum to document progress and produce the data that *will* be believed by those who are both our customers and our employers.

Acknowledgments

This book is dedicated to my husband, Lee F. Olsen, a true partner who shares all things with me—his perspectives on 30 years in school administration; his help with every mundane task pulling this project together; and, most essential, his loving support and encouragement.

Special thanks are owed to Dave Pedersen, our friend and super-techie, who patiently constructed graphs and visual organizers that illuminate this text.

Without the dedication and cooperation of committed educators who were willing to take risks with me, there would be nothing to write and no examples to provide. I am grateful to hundreds of named and unnamed teachers, principals, and district administrators whose stories are told in this text.

Beyond gratitude, I express my admiration for the leadership shared by:

Mr. Gary Bersell, Director of Instructional Services, Janesville, Wisconsin

Dr. Lois Brick, North Central Association of Colleges and Schools and Wisconsin Department of Public Instruction

Mr. Cal Callaway, Director of Instruction, Oregon, Wisconsin

Dr. Sara Larsen, Director of Instruction, East Troy, Wisconsin

Dr. Mabel Schumacher, Director of Instruction, Fort Atkinson, Wisconsin

Dr. Sandra Sorrell, Director of Curriculum, Instruction and Assessment, Poudre School District, Fort Collins, Colorado

Watching these *people* work with *passion* is all the *proof* I need that public education is in good hands.

About the Author

Edie L. Holcomb currently serves as Director of Standards and Assessment for Seattle Public Schools. She is highly regarded for her ability to link research and practice on issues related to school leadership, improvement, and reform. Her background includes teaching experience at all grade levels and administrative experience at the building and district level in Illinois, Alabama, Minnesota, South Dakota, Iowa, and Wisconsin. Her work in the Lewis Central School District of Council Bluffs, Iowa, was granted the Excellence in Staff Development Award by the Iowa Association for Supervision and Curriculum Development in 1988.

Holcomb holds a BS in elementary education, an MS in gifted education, and an EdS and PhD in educational administration. Her dissertation on the needs of beginning principals, completed at the University of Minnesota, received the Paul F. Salmon Award for Outstanding Education Leadership Research from the American Association of School Administrators in 1990.

Holcomb served as Associate Director of the National Center for Effective Schools, developing *School-Based Instructional Leadership*, a training program for site-based teams now disseminated through Phi Delta Kappa International. She has provided technical assistance for implementation of school improvement efforts throughout the United States and in Canada, Guam, St. Lucia, and Hong Kong. Her first book, *Asking the Right Questions: Tools and Techniques for Teamwork,* is currently in its fourth printing. She consults on school improvement, professional development and systemic implementation of standards-based education. She can be contacted directly at 360-671-1164 or elholcomb@aol.com.

1

Using Data to Align School Improvement

"Well, lady, there's good news and bad news. Which do you want first?" This was not the opening line of a comic. It was the greeting of the mechanic as he returned from the service bay of the dealership where I had purchased my still-pretty-new red sports car. True to my Calvinistic upbringing, I asked for the bad news first. "You're going to need four new tires, and the high-performance type you have are not included in the special sale we're running. You also need your front end aligned and your brake pads are nearly shot. You're looking at right around a grand altogether."

My treat-the-mechanic-nice-or-it-will-only-get-worse smile faded as my heart sank and my stomach somersaulted. I could see my little vacation nest egg fading before my eyes. "So what could possibly be the good news?"

I wished I hadn't asked. It was all the spark he needed to fire up a lecture that seemed prerecorded for female customers. "Lady, the good news is that you're alive. I can't figure out why you women can't seem to grasp the importance of basic routine maintenance. You hit something or something hit you and knocked that front end out of line and instead of getting it checked and fixed right away, you just let it go on and on until your tires are worn all uneven and the right front one could have blown out any time and put you into a skid or a rollover, and with your brake drums affected, too, you'd have a mighty hard time driving your way out of it. Anybody who'd neglect a car like this shouldn't be allowed to have one in the first place. Didn't anyone ever tell you the number one rule of owning a car? Take good care of your car and it will take good care of you! You're just lucky you got in here when you did!"

What an embarrassing, expensive experience for someone who uses the word *alignment* almost daily in her organizational development work! There's no way to calculate the number of school improvement/reform/ restructuring/transformation efforts that have gone out of control, rolled over, or skidded to a stop due to lack of alignment. Well-intended but misaligned efforts result in disillusioned educators who resolve, "Never again"; disappointed constituents who wonder, "Why can't we get our act together?"; and disengaged or disenfranchised students moving through a system of public education without having truly learned.

Figure 1.1 illustrates the relationships that must be in alignment so that investments of human and fiscal resources will pay dividends of improved student achievement. This figure is a composite of the key components of a variety of change processes used in school districts I have known: Effective Schools models, school improvement accreditation processes, total quality management, and strategic planning, to name a few. I have frequently seen one or two components done well. I have rarely seen a fully aligned system. But I have observed that the districts with the most tightly aligned and data-driven approaches to change and improvement are also those making a difference in student achievement.

This visual organizer of school improvement will appear twice in this chapter. First, we will explore the relationships among the components; then we will describe the importance of using data at critical points in the school improvement process (Figure 1.2).

Alignment Between Mission and the School Portfolio

The literature on change is full of materials that stress the importance of an organization having a statement or document that articulates its "passion"— the core values and purposes that guide it. Few authors describe the mission as a set of commitments for which the organization is accountable. The vertical arrow between the Mission and the School Portfolio demonstrates the need to provide evidence that the mission is being fulfilled.

The term *school portfolio* is used here to describe a collection of data compiled at the individual school level. Chapters 5 and 6 discuss its contents and format. Although it is frequently referred to as a *profile*, I prefer to call it a school portfolio for three reasons. First, I believe that the comparison to a portfolio of student work is very fitting because of the school context. Second, the term *portfolio* is apt because a student's (or artist's) portfolio is intended to demonstrate three important aspects of his or her work: the range of skills, the very best products, and artifacts that provide evidence of progress and learning. A school also needs to present the wide variety of needs it addresses,

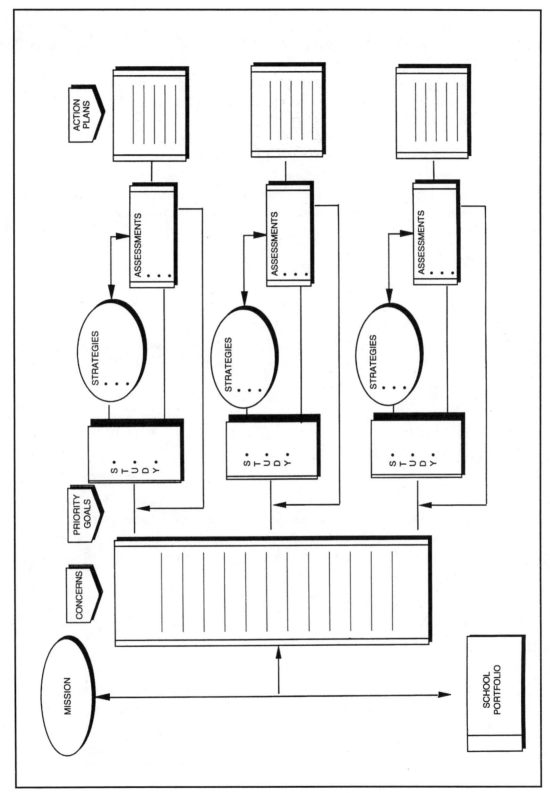

Figure 1.1. Aligning School Improvement

3

examples of success to celebrate, and evidence of improvement occurring where needed.

Third, I believe one of the reasons school-level data should be compiled is to paint a more complete picture of the uniqueness of that school and its students than the term profile implies. Painting a picture requires more than an outline or silhouette. This is not to say that a school portfolio should be a two-ton tome. Chapter 5 will emphasize the need to be selective about its contents, so staff and constituents are not overwhelmed and intimidated by sheer volume.

The relationship between the mission and the school portfolio is that one should provide evidence of the other. In organizational development terminology, it's looking for alignment between our "espoused theories" (beliefs) and our "theories in use" (how we operate on a daily basis).[1] When we provide evidence of what we do, how closely does it match what we say?

Alignment Among Mission, Portfolio, and Concerns

The length of the vertical arrow represents the amount of discrepancy between rhetoric and reality. Awareness of this discrepancy should generate a range of concerns, which Peter Senge might describe as "creative tension."[2] This relationship is shown by the horizontal arrow.

Alignment Between Concerns and Priority Goals

Many concerns may arise, but only a few can be addressed with the type of substantive, systemic effort needed to change student achievement. The contrast between the many lines in the "Concerns" box and only three spaces for "Priority Goals" represents the need to focus on a few top priorities. Chapter 8 describes how and why this is so important.

Alignment Between Goals and Strategies

Too often, participants in a school improvement process have unrealistic time expectations placed on them. They may be asked to set goals each year and be given just a day to go on retreat and develop the improvement plan. This model yields several unintended, undesired consequences. Significant needs are not addressed as goals, because they can't be attained in one year. Strategies for meeting the goals are brainstormed based on the particular experiences and preferences of the group, without careful study of research and best practice. Important factors in the local context that would inform these decisions are ignored. The vertical box called "Study" represents a barrier and is intended to communicate the need to stop and learn more before deciding "what to do about it." The first bullet in the Study box represents the need to further analyze and better understand the problem area (see Chapter 9). The second bullet reminds us to investigate suggested strategies and identify those that are proven practices with documented success increasing student learning.

Problem Identified.

Alignment Between
Goals and Assessments

The Study box includes a third bullet, which represents the need to learn how to document progress toward attainment of the goal. Traditional methods of program evaluation and school improvement have claimed success by reporting evidence that selected strategies were implemented. Glowing accounts are provided of the number of teachers who attended training and the number of new initiatives begun. Only recently has the emphasis switched to documentation of what happens differently for students and what they now know and do that they previously didn't know or do.

One reason we so often reported what the adults did, rather than the results achieved for students, is that it was easier to do the former because we knew how. This is why the third bullet in the Study box represents the need to develop greater assessment literacy and a view of assessment that is broader than our reflex definition, "Tests."

It is important to note that there are also three bullets in the oval labeled "Strategies" and in the rectangle labeled "Assessments." These bullets do not represent three specific issues as the three bullets in the Study box do. What they illustrate is that a goal can rarely be met by only one strategy and attainment of a goal can rarely be documented using only one measure. The need for multiple measures is addressed further in Chapter 10.

Alignment Among Goals,
Strategies, and Assessments

The arrows among Priority Goals, Strategies, and Assessments are intended to imply a cyclical or circular relationship. This process is not as straightforward as the two-dimensional confines of print make it appear. For example, the two-way arrow between Strategies and Assessments reminds us that determining what evidence we need and learning how to gather it will also inform what we need to do as strategies so the evidence we seek will be available. As a matter of fact, when I work with planning groups, I often restrict them from discussing strategies until they have a good idea what documentation of goal attainment would look like. In Chapters 3, 4, and 9, we describe evidence as indicators that are either measurable or observable in the school setting.

Alignment Among Strategies, Assessments, and Action Plans

"Action Plans" include the detailed steps necessary to guide implementation of both the selected strategies to create improvement and the procedures by which evidence of improvement will be compiled. Based on my observations, I think one reason we have so little to show for our efforts is that we don't plan how to get the "proof." We get all the way to the end of a process and then scramble for any kind of "post" information we can get our hands on.

The number of Action Plan lines is not precise, but the message is this. If we have courageously adopted substantive, systemic goals and selected multiple strategies and assessments, it's not likely that the steps needed to carry out these decisions can be developed in sufficient detail all on one planning sheet.

Using Data to Create Alignment

The auto mechanic who worked on my car had a computer and a number of other tools he used to get my front end aligned and wheels back in balance. The tool for aligning our school improvement process is data. On Figure 1.2, the critical points for use of data are superimposed on the basic diagram from Figure 1.1. The initial version of the school portfolio is clarified as baseline data. Shaded arrows have been added to illustrate how the school portfolio continually expands as more data is acquired and used throughout the process. These arrows show how the regular use of data changes the appearance of a linear process into a continuous improvement cycle.

Baseline Data

When most schools make the commitment to become more data-driven, they are panic-stricken about where they are going to find information to include. Then they discover that there are "mother lodes" of data scattered throughout the school and district that have been as shrouded with mystery as the lost ark and certainly have never been mined. Once people begin to discover what they *could* include in the initial school portfolio, it becomes a challenge to limit its size and scope. Chapter 5 provides some ideas for focusing the baseline school portfolio. The shaded arrows on Figure 1.2 illustrate why it's so essential. The school portfolio is a work in progress at all times, and there will be ample opportunities to add more information or more detailed analysis as the process continues.

Focusing Data

Data is one of three filters used in Chapter 8 to help the school focus on a limited number of top priority goals. This is a critical point, because it

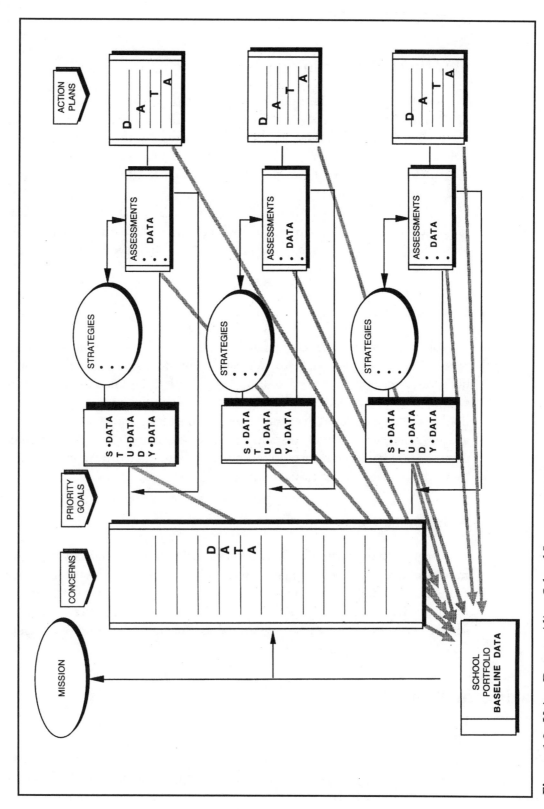

Figure 1.2. Using Data to Align School Improvement

establishes the awareness that the school portfolio was not just something "finished and done with" but something that will be used regularly whenever decisions are pending.

Studying Before Acting

The three bullets in the Study box represented further analysis of the issue or need, investigation of research and best practice, and improvement of assessment literacy. All of these involve data. Analysis of the existing situation may include further analysis of existing data or collection of additional data. The shaded arrow shows how this data becomes part of the school portfolio as it is continually updated.

When new strategies are being selected, data that substantiate their claims of effectiveness should be a prerequisite. Deciding and learning how to assess attainment of the goals is learning how to amass data needed to document progress.

Designing Data

As improvement goals are crafted into language that will motivate whole-school effort, the question, "How will we know we're getting there?" should be addressed. Some answers will be very evident, because there are data sources that were already available and were used in the initial school portfolio that can be monitored over time. Standardized tests and state assessments are two examples. Other answers will have to be constructed as professionals discuss what could be measured, observed, or aggregated from information they already keep as individual teachers.

Monitoring Data

Chapter 10 discusses data collection as implementation takes place. This may be of two types. Assessments have already been identified for use when monitoring student performance. It may also be wise to collect data that verify the use of selected strategies. As these data are collected, they are added to the school portfolio, creating a stronger database for the next round of analysis, goal setting, and improvement.

Engaging the People

Although this introductory chapter has focused on the data themselves, this book is really about *people:* how they feel about data; what they do (or don't do) with data; why they don't; and how to help them get into it, get used to it, and end up liking it. The people we're talking about are the full range of interested parties frequently called *stakeholders.* The school improvement process should be open and participatory, involving teachers, administrators, support staff, students, parents, community representatives, and business partners in a variety of ways. For convenience, I have shortened the list by using two inclusive terms. In this book, the word *staff* refers to all the adults who work in the school, whether they are licensed teachers, aides, clerical staff, or administrators. I use the term *constituents* to refer to the interested adult parties outside the school, including parents and community members. The word *students* speaks for itself. I have kept them in their own category because I believe they are the most intimately involved with and aware of the school's needs and successes at the same time that they are least integrated into analysis, decision-making, and planning processes.

I will coin one additional term, which refers to getting people engaged with data—*ad hocracy*. In district after district, I have been asked how to recruit community members and engage parents and the community in this process. My own study of implementation following training of school leadership teams verified that participation by community members seems to drop off after the mission is written and goals are set.[3] As a result, I have placed less emphasis on standing committees and greater reliance on ad hoc task groups. Standing committees have a limited number of slots available for constituents and demand a long-range commitment. A series of ad hoc groups, each with a specific task and a defined time commitment, can provide opportunities for many more participants, can attract those with interest and expertise to apply to just one aspect of the process, and can make it easier to recruit busy people when they know they aren't "signing on for life."

Staff in Particular

The only role group whose members are or may feel they are "lifers" are the school's staff, especially the teachers. Although the entire school improvement process should be participatory and decision making should be shared, teachers must be given special status in the actual gathering and analysis of data. Chapter 3 lists several reasons why this is new, unfamiliar, uncomfortable work. Leaders should be sensitive to these feelings and provide shelter for teachers—not to shield them from the data, but to provide a safe environment for their explorations. All constituents have a right of access to data, but teachers should have first chance to explore and analyze and prepare to discuss it with others.

Ownership

Many schools and districts operate as though there is another inch on the right-hand side of Figure 1.1, with a last step called "Get Buy-In." A small team carries out the process, sets goals, develops plans, and "delivers" them in final form to be accepted by the rest. Then I get the phone calls about how no one seems to be really "doing the strategies" and will I come help them convince the staff to "buy in." First, I have a personal hang-up about the word *buy*. Educators are not gullible consumers who will latch on to something if you just attach the right incentive or make the right "deal." I prefer to talk about ownership, not as something purchased, but as something grown, crafted, or invented. You can "buy" something in a day, but you can only grow, craft, or invent something over time. Ownership must be created along the way through involvement and communication at every step. That is why the activities described in this book are designed to engage the whole staff all at once, rather than rely too much on a team or training of trainers model.

Getting Started

The first activity should be an overview for all staff that includes the concepts in this chapter and provides a "big picture" sense of the overall process. Although the essential first audience is staff, the same information should be made available to other constituents through invitation to the general session, special meetings, or written communication. Chapter 11 describes a district's "Data Day," which begins with this type of general overview.

On the Road Again

My tires are now replaced and balanced, my front end is aligned, and my car is tracking straight down the road. If the components of school improvement are aligned with data, the school should also be able to move ahead and see its forward progress. In the next two chapters, we'll explore why the use of data is becoming more and more essential, yet seems so unengaging.

Notes

1. Argyris, C., & Schon, D. A. (1974). *Theory in practice: Increasing professional effectiveness.* San Francisco: Jossey-Bass.

2. Senge, P. (1990). *The fifth discipline: The art and practice of the learning organization.* New York: Doubleday.

3. Holcomb, E. L. (1995). To implement together, train together. *Journal of Staff Development, 16,* 59-64.

2

Why Bother to Get Engaged With Data?

Public demands for accountability are motivating increased awareness of the need to provide evidence of a school's effectiveness. School boards are requiring schools to demonstrate how they use data to guide decision making and plan their improvement efforts. Even accreditation requirements are moving from an input model of verifying factors like adequate resources and qualified staff to an output model focused on evidence of student success. Reauthorization of federal funds has emphasized the need to use proven programs and approaches and document improvements in student achievement. Public school choice is a reality in an increasing number of states, and some states are even funneling tax funds into vouchers for students to attend private schools. Public education is a service industry that must be user friendly or lose its market share to vouchers, private schools, and for-profit enterprises.

These factors create an undeniable need for schools and districts to demonstrate the results they achieve for their students and constituents, but they are also perceived as outside threats to educators. Mandates and competition don't kindle enough enthusiasm and energy to learn the new skills needed for these unfamiliar tasks and to complete the extra work. A more personal meaning must be created as motivation to work with data. The activities in this chapter have been successfully used to help people generate the passion needed to produce the proof.

The Motivation Continuum

Educators are familiar with the terminology of *intrinsic* (or internal) motivation and *extrinsic* (or external) motivation. Most would agree that intrinsic motivation is the more powerful force for change. This activity allows participants to choose factors that create meaning and motivation for each of them as individuals. There are two versions of the "Motivation Continuum" activity that can be further adapted depending on the group.

The Reflective Continuum

The first version is best suited for occasions when the audience can work in small groups and is open to reflection and serious discussion with peers. It takes about 15 to 20 minutes to complete. Each group of three to five participants needs a blank form like that presented in Figure 2.1. This form may be produced on 8.5-by-11-inch paper for each participant or each group can use large chart paper and markers to create a joint product. A supply of stick-on notes may also come in handy.

First, ask individual participants to think about the question, "Why is it important to be able to produce evidence of what the school achieves for its students?" If they are using individual worksheets, they may write directly on them. Or each participant can have a supply of stick-on notes and write one of the factors he or she identifies on each note.

After generating reasons why the use of data is increasingly important, have participants arrange the factors they identified along their own worksheet or on the large chart. They should discuss the degree to which each factor is driven by outside forces or arises from internally perceived needs and desires. Figure 2.2 shows the factors identified by a group in a recent workshop.

After time has been allowed for discussion, ask participants whether any of these factors seem inappropriate or unfair. Acknowledge that it's perfectly all right to feel this way, and tell them to cross out the reasons that feel *demotivating*. Then have participants circle or star the factors on their own continuum that they find meaningful. These are the sources that will provide motivation for their ongoing exploration of data.

 Conclude the activity by asking each participant to make a one-sentence response to a prompt such as, "I can be motivated to work with our data if I remember that . . . " These statements are the first level of commitment to get engaged with data.

The "Live" Motivation Continuum

To be successful with the first version of the Motivation Continuum, the facilitator needs to be confident of the group's willingness to be reflective. Sometimes the facilitator is not that familiar with the group or the group is simply too large for that approach. This is a variation that takes about 20 minutes and has been used successfully with as many as 200 teachers in an

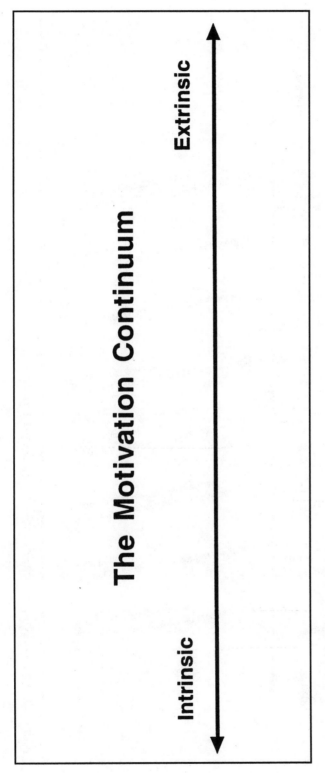

Figure 2.1. The Motivation Continuum

13

14

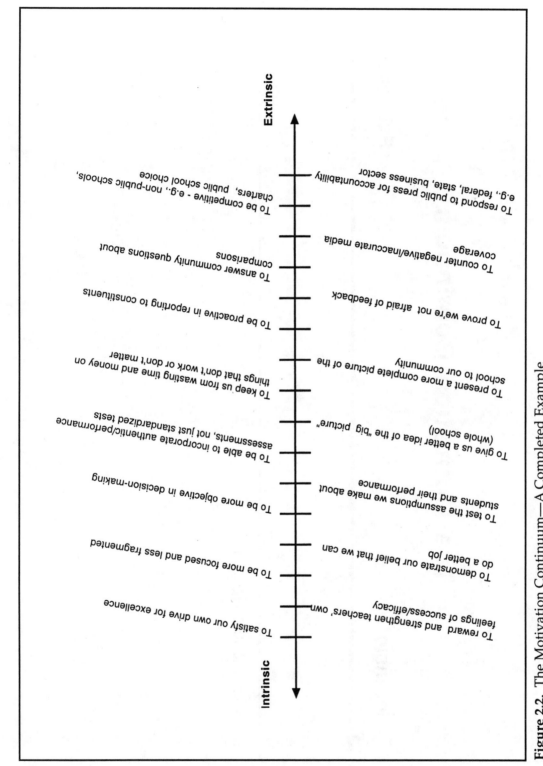

Figure 2.2. The Motivation Continuum—A Completed Example

auditorium setting. It even worked with a group of 85 high school teachers on the Friday afternoon before Christmas vacation!

Instead of having participants work in small groups to generate the reasons to get engaged with data, this variation starts with factors previously identified in other groups, such as those in Figure 2.2. In preparation, print these factors in bold colors on strips of chart paper. Also prepare two signs: one saying "Extrinsic" and one saying "Intrinsic."

Tell the audience that you have been working with teachers in other schools and have brought their ideas about using data to get this group's reaction. Describe this as an audience participation game show, where audience members will need to be active, loud, and demanding to succeed.

Ask for two volunteers or recruits from the crowd who are willing to accept completely menial tasks and leave more complex assignments to others. Give these two the "Extrinsic" and "Intrinsic" signs and ask them to stand at opposite ends of the front of the room. Briefly review the two terms as they relate to motivation, and recruit individuals to hold the strips of paper on which you printed the factors from Figure 2.2. The responsibility of the audience is to scream, yell, and gesture at their colleagues to tell them where to stand so the factors they represent are in order across the room based on their extrinsic or intrinsic value.

Most audiences relish the rare permission to be rowdy at an in-service and participate readily in the true spirit of "The Price Is Right." If people hesitate, humor them with comments like, "Isn't there someone up there you always wanted to tell where to go? Now's your chance." Or goad them a little with, "Don't tell me you just want to 'sit and git'?!"

After the audience members have arranged their colleagues along the live continuum, use another game show adaptation called the "Applause-o-Meter." At least a few in the group will remember winners being chosen by the length and volume of the applause. Tell the audience that it will now rate the motivational power of these factors. Participants can be silent or boo and hiss at factors they reject and clap and whistle for those they accept as meaningful reasons to get more engaged with data. As you move along the continuum, have the factors that are validated step forward.

Conclude by briefly commenting on the importance of each of the factors the group validated as meaningful. Ask the group members to get a mental picture of their colleagues holding these words and remember that these are the real reasons they will be working more with data in the days to come. On one district's Data Day (Chapter 11), photos were taken for a district publication and the "lineup" of reasons to use data became a matter of record for future reference during school improvement activities.

No, the List Won't Work

Every time I have used this activity with a group, someone has requested a copy of the list of factors to take home and distribute. Distributing the list—

or displaying it on a transparency—is not a successful variation of the Motivation Continuum. Intrinsic motivation must be nurtured. It can't be bestowed.

Swapping Stories

Among the items in Figure 2.2 are "to present a more complete picture of the school to our community" and "to give us a better idea of the 'big picture'" of the whole school. Another phrasing would be, "So we can tell our own story."

This activity helps build motivation by providing examples of the kind of stories most schools would like to report. Gather examples from case studies and books you have read that describe school improvement efforts with documented results. One excellent source is Mike Schmoker's book *Results: The Key to Continuous Improvement*,[1] in which he reports many success stories such as the following:

> The bright side of collegiality can be found at Northview Elementary School in Manhattan, Kansas. Students realized huge gains between 1983 and 1989, when teachers began to collaborate. In reading, 4th and 6th grade scores on district achievement tests rose from 59 to 100 percent, and from 41 to 97 percent, respectively. In math, 4th grade scores rose from 70 to 100 percent; 6th grade scores, from 31 to 97 percent. How? Principal Dan Yunk began to arrange for teams of teachers to meet routinely to analyze scores, identify strengths and weaknesses, and develop ways to effectively address them. (pp. 14-15)

> At Adlai E. Stevenson High School in Lincolnshire, Illinois, teacher teams meet once a month to collaborate, and analyze results at least four times a year. . . . In 1985, before the process was introduced, the school did not rank at all in the top 50 schools in the 13-state Midwest region. In 1992, when goals were established and collaborative time was instituted, the school ranked first in the region, and by 1994, it was among the top 20 schools in the world. . . . Last year, the school established new records in every traditional indicator of student achievement, including grade distributions, failure rates, average ACT scores, average SAT scores, percentage of honor grades on Advanced Placement examinations, and average scores in each of the five areas of the state achievement tests. (pp. 15-16)

> A middle school in Richmond County, Georgia, had instituted measures to help at-risk students: lower class size, special programs, and counseling. Nothing happened. It was not until teachers began to meet in study groups to help each other implement more effective teaching strategies that results came. In one year, the average student went from making 6 months' progress to making 10 months' progress. The promotion rate increased from 30 to 70 percent. The following year, it increased again—to 95 percent. (p. 21)

Prepare several of these excerpts in large font on separate sheets of paper. Identify "news reporters" and—if your room setup allows—have them sit on stools behind a table or podium to give the impression of a news broadcast. One way to follow each story is to ask the audience, "What role did data play in being able to report this news?" Other questions may be:

◆ Would you like to be able to report this news about your school?

◆ What were the key factors that made these gains possible?

◆ Let's hear how it would sound if it was the story of your school. Have the "reporters" read the story again, substituting the name of their school in the text.

◆ What success story do you want to be able to tell about your school? Ask each participant do a "Quick-Write"[2] of three to five sentences, but call it a sound bite they wish they'd hear on their local station. A few of these can be read aloud to the group. Collect and save these "desired stories" for future use, such as

— Creating a collage of them on a bulletin board in the teachers' lounge
— Referring to them as starting points if the school has work to do on its mission
— Reading one or two of them as warmups at each faculty meeting or work session that involves data and school improvement

Roles of Staff, Students, and Constituents

The process of school improvement needs the combined work of staff, students, and parents. The activities in this chapter are designed primarily to engage staff, but can certainly be used with any group. As Chapter 3 points out, the use of data presents new challenges and the adults in the school have a lot at stake. Students and parents do not have as much need for these particular activities and may even wonder why the use of data isn't just taken for granted by their teachers.

Notes

1. Schmoker, M. (1996). *Results: The key to continuous improvement.* Alexandria, VA: Association for Supervision and Curriculum Development.

2. Holcomb, E. L. (1996). *Asking the right questions: Tools and techniques for teamwork.* Thousand Oaks, CA: Corwin. See pages 90-92 for a description of the Quick-Write activity.

3

The Status of Data Use
(or Nonuse)

Through activities like those described in Chapter 2, educators acknowledge the need for proof of a school's effectiveness. But that doesn't mean they know how to go about providing it. For the past 2 years, I have enjoyed being the consultant for a consortium of school districts using Goals 2000 funds to design and implement a collaborative school improvement model. Sixteen districts participated during the design year, and another 12 districts reviewed the model and joined the consortium for implementation. The districts range in size from 16 schools to 1 K-8 unit, with a total of 93 schools participating. Along with my experiences throughout Wisconsin and in several other states, my work with this group has influenced my perceptions about data use in schools.

During the first year of the consortium, focus groups were conducted in the districts to determine their status with regard to use of data and the degree to which data influenced their goals and those goals influenced school and classroom activity. Figure 3.1 reports the types of data most frequently mentioned in answer to the question, "What data about student achievement do you currently use?"

The most frequently mentioned types of data were results from the state assessments of reading at the 3rd-grade level and the 4th-, 8th-, and 10th-grade knowledge and concepts tests. One of the 16 districts did not submit the focus group transcripts, which means that 2 of the 15 reporting districts did not even

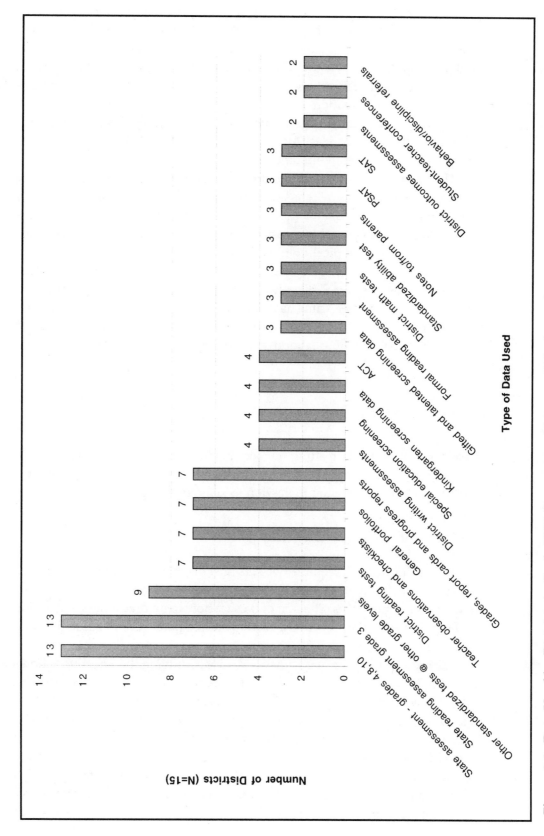

Figure 3.1. Data Used by Districts in Goals 2000 Consortium (does not include single response items)

mention the state assessments during the conversation. It may be that they were simply assumed to be included automatically or—from comments I heard at other times—the participants may still have been thinking, "This too shall pass" and didn't acknowledge them. Single-item responses that were not displayed in Figure 3.1 include other performance assessment, career portfolios, student self-evaluation, individual goal-setting, timed tests, assignment books, class rank, number of graduates, pass-fail lists, Honor Roll, cumulative folders, health concerns lists, Advanced Placement tests, ASVAB, EXPLORE, and postsecondary follow-up data.

The pareto chart in Figure 3.2 displays information about *how* participants reported *using* the data. Wisconsin traditionally receives high ratings in state education comparisons, and these districts score in the mid-range of state rankings. They are not problem districts. So it is disappointing to note that the use of data in these typical districts in a progressive education state is still primarily for sorting and selecting into special programs and classes such as Applied English, Study Skills, and "general education track." Reporting to parents, a legal mandate, came next in frequency. Less than half of the districts had any participant comment on using data at the classroom level, and there was no mention at all of collaborative schoolwide planning for improvement. Why might this be?

Reasons for Resistance to Data

Based on my research, reading, personal conversations with school leaders, and observations, I suggest six reasons why data are little used and why it is so difficult to generate enough passion to get people engaged with the proof.

1. Lack of (Proper) Training

Improving schools requires two sets of skills that few school leaders have had the opportunity to acquire in their graduate work or have seen modeled in their own experiences. The first of these is how to involve others in decision making. The second is how to use data in appropriate ways to guide the decision making.

It's been 14 years since, as a new principal studying the Effective Schools research, I began trying to engage staff in collegial discussion of data about our school. It was a real struggle, and I tried to figure out why. I wondered if it was a task I shouldn't have tackled with them, or if I was going about it all wrong, or if the staff members just weren't as qualified as I expected them to be. I even checked to see if I had as many teachers with master's degrees as the other schools did. Looking back, I realize that my facilitation skills were probably lacking, but I believe even more strongly that collegial discussion of data is a task that must be undertaken and I'm much more aware of the amount

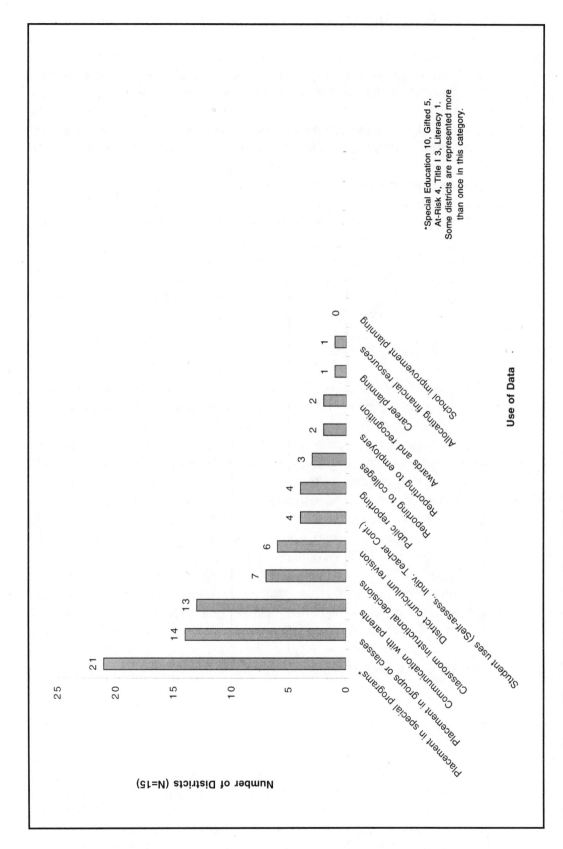

Figure 3.2. Uses of Data by Districts in Goals 2000 Consortium

21

of professional development and support that is needed to have the task accepted.

This book isn't an analysis of graduate programs in education and educational administration. That's been done already. My observations are that more than half of our teachers have graduate degrees and have taken at least one course in tests and measurements or statistics. I have four graduate degrees myself and can recall no class discussion of what to do with assessment information in planning how to help the students do better. I have come to the conclusion that such courses are taught by researchers as though they are preparing researchers. As a result, the emphasis is on esoteric experimental design—which can't be replicated in a normal school setting—and use of empirical data unlike the types of data listed in Figure 3.1. Gerald Bracey agrees that

> many of the university professors who create and use statistics are more comfortable using them than they are teaching other human beings what they mean. And in all too many instances, statistics are taught in a theoretically rarefied atmosphere replete with hard-to-understand formulas and too few examples relevant to the daily life of education practitioners.[1]

It *is* important to know whether a research study was conducted in such a way that it should be believed and its findings applied. It *is* important for students pursuing the terminal degree to conduct a rigorous study as a demonstration that they can properly apply the concepts of good research. But a considerable number of doctoral degrees belong to practitioners who will need to use data in vastly different ways.

The uses of data suggested in this book would not meet the academic rigor of a dissertation. That is not their purpose. Our purpose is to create readiness to try simple things, so we can experience success and see value in using data and then have the will to gain more sophisticated skills.

The unfortunate reality is that the data-related training teachers have had becomes a barrier rather than an asset. As comments later in the chapter indicate, most of us hated the course, feel we barely passed, and learned just enough to think that any use of data we can fit into a regular school routine must be suspect. It's not just what we have to learn that's the challenge—it's what we have to *un*learn.

2. Lack of Time

A common factor in all three success stories quoted in Chapter 2 was time—not just free time for individual planning and preparation, but time to work collaboratively. When we're overwhelmed with the list of things we know we *should* do, we resort to completing the things we know we *can* do. It's the only way we have even a shot at maintaining the illusion that we're in control of our lives. In Chapter 10, we share some ideas for finding time.

3. Feast or Famine

When a school begins its efforts to become more results oriented, there are two times when participants are likely to hit the panic button, and I can usually predict when they are going to occur. The first is when we talk—as we do here in Chapters 4 and 5—about the kinds of information we want to know and be able to use. About the time a tentative list has been drafted, the blood drains from the faces of the participants and they look at me in horror. "Where are we going to *get* all of this?!" Then we begin to identify where each kind of data is now housed, who has access and will retrieve it, and so forth.

A month or so later, we get together again. Now we have the desired data—and all the other information that has been uncovered in the meantime—and the faces are flushed with anxiety. "What are we going to *do* with all of this?!" For this reason, I recommend that the initial school portfolio contain a carefully selected, limited number of data sources that the entire staff can review and discuss. (See Chapter 7.)

4. Fear of Evaluation

The greatest conundrum I've encountered in my attempts to help schools use data is the fear expressed in questions like, "How can we keep this from being used against us?" and "Why would I want to help create the hatchet they use to give me the ax?" This is particularly puzzling since no one has been able to give me one example of a person dismissed from his or her teaching position based on performance of students. (As a matter of fact, few can remember anyone ever being fired for *any* reason.)

5. Fear of Exposure

I have come to believe that the expressed fear of evaluation may be a cover for the more valid anxiety that our inadequacies will be exposed if we try something new that we realize we should know. I experience this myself when I am around people who are current and confident with their technology skills. Regardless of whether these are separate fears or one, they are real and they interfere with trying new things.

6. Confusing a Technical Problem With a Cultural Problem

When we ask teachers to look at evidence of their school's effectiveness, we are not just asking them to crunch numbers and plot graphs. That's the technical part. The reality is that we are challenging the existing culture.

Schools have been characterized by individualization and isolation, described as a set of individual enterprises bound together by a common parking lot. If there are "shopping mall" high schools, there are also "strip mall" elementary schools.

Working collaboratively with data is essential to accepting collective responsibility for the learning of students during their total time at that school. The barriers that have to fall are not just barriers of lack of training. Cultural norms like "Let me close my classroom door and do my own thing" have to be replaced by more systemic thinking.

Soothing the Limbic System

I am just beginning to understand the brain research that should enlighten our instructional approaches and make us more effective with children.[2] The power of the limbic system to override both rational thought and basic bodily functions is awesome. As the emotional center of our brain, the limbic system relays stimuli to the neocortex where reasoning and planning take place. Since the limbic system influences what we pay attention to, consider important, and remember, we must ease anxiety and reduce stress when we challenge people to get engaged with data. Facilitators of cultural change need to be skillful users of language, stories, humor, and music as ways to soothe the limbic system. The next three activities are designed to achieve that goal.

Our Own Thesaurus

Many years ago in another lifetime in another world (it seems), I taught first grade. One of the ways we learned to use language was by making individual word booklets that were called "My Own Dictionary." That's where I got the title for this activity, and the concept is the same.

To communicate and work together, we need to agree on what we will call the things that we do. We have often helped create our own Frankenstein monster as the "last year's new thing—this year's new thing—next year's new thing" phenomenon. We bring an additional component to strengthen an existing process, but we also transport a whole set of terms for it that make it sound like something entirely foreign. Then our colleagues wonder what happened to the other way, because it had its own and separate language. This activity is designed to be used at the beginning of a new program or process to help everyone acquire a common vocabulary and create a consistency of language that provides continuity and reduces miscommunication.

In preparation, list terms that are part of the new approach on a flip chart, leaving plenty of space between them. The first step is to go through the list with the group, asking participants to name as many adjectives as they can for each term. Repeat each word and record it. It's helpful to ask someone else to serve as recorder, so you can observe nonverbals during this part of the process. You will note some interesting reactions to words that some people assume mean the same thing and other participants don't think are the same thing at all.

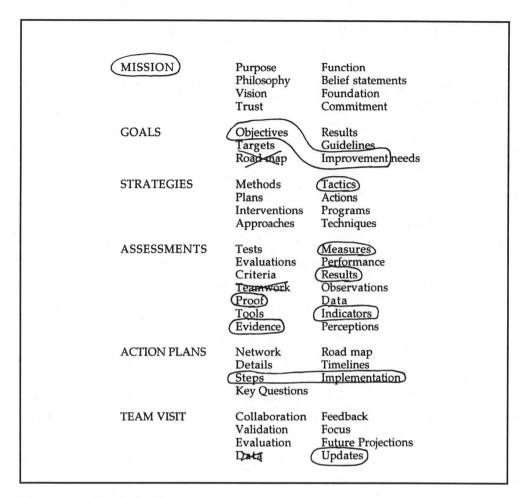

Figure 3.3. Our Own Thesaurus

After the "thesaurus" has been generated, go back through each term and ask the group to discuss language that has been used in the past. Encourage participants to focus also on the connotations that have become attached to certain words. Sometimes people will realize they've thought they disagreed for years when they simply had different definitions for terms they were both using.

Complete the activity by asking group members to select those terms that sound familiar and have positive connotations in their setting and agree to use them consistently. Figure 3.3 shows the product of this activity when the group was blending the vocabulary of its strategic planning process with the terminology of accreditation by the North Central Association of Colleges and Schools. The result was agreement on a single term for each of five components, with an intentional decision to use *many* words for assessment so participants would expand their horizons beyond the automatic association with "tests." Some words were crossed out because they had appeared in more than one place and the group decided to avoid them because they could cause confusion.

Warming Up to Data

At the start of workshops that relate to data or work on the school portfolio, I ask people to introduce themselves with the usual name, position, and school and complete this sentence:

When I think about data and graphs,

I feel like (a) _____

because _____.

Here is a sample of typical responses:

- ◆ I feel helpless because what we have is not very good.
- ◆ I feel excited because this will strengthen what we have.
- ◆ I feel like an owl because I'm wondering "who-who-who's" gonna do this.
- ◆ I feel like I'm in a stats course and wonder if I'm supposed to make the numbers lie for our benefit.
- ◆ I feel like a computer because this will be dehumanizing people.
- ◆ I feel like I'm in the wrong room because I noticed the accountants are meeting next door.
- ◆ I feel like I'm on "Price Is Right" because something's hidden behind every door.
- ◆ I feel like a deer in the headlights because I don't know which way to run.
- ◆ I feel like I'm at the edge of a minefield with a long stick because there's so much negative reaction and doesn't seem to be much appreciation of what we do well and how hard we work.
- ◆ I feel like a professional because I can finally use the math skills I teach to help my whole school.
- ◆ I feel like Marcia Clark because I've got all kinds of evidence and the jury (my teachers) just won't believe it.
- ◆ I finally feel like I belong because I hate touchy-feely workshops and it looks like we're going to do real work here.

During the introductions, capture some of these on the flip chart. If the room setup allows, it's even more effective to jot some of them down on a notepad as you walk around the room. This allows you to observe nonverbals and chuckle to yourself at the shocked looks on many faces when someone says he or she *likes* working with data. After the introductions, respond to some of them. For example, you can reassure the "statistaphobics" that we will be doing nothing more complicated than counting, percentages, and simple graphing so if they have fifth-grade math skills, they will be fine. You will also have a chance to diagnose the levels of readiness of the group and adjust accordingly throughout the day.

Since participants usually attend as members of a team from a school, I also use this activity to check the composition of the group. If there is just one of the "excited" type at each table, I can be fairly sure the day will go smoothly. When all the members of a team express anxiety, I ask them if they know someone back at their school who would probably answer the prompt with enthusiasm. Usually they do, and I suggest that they recruit that person to help with this part of their school improvement process.

Cheers and Jeers

"Cheers and Jeers" is an activity that provides an opportunity to use music and humor to relax and release tension. Ask participants to work in groups of three or four or as table groups, depending on the room setup. Their job is to create a cheer or jeer (depending on how they feel about using data). These can be performed all at once, or you can call on one table at a time throughout a full-day workshop when the group needs an energizer. People will actually work through breaks and lunch on their cheer or jeer, which raises the level of energy throughout the room. Here are some cheers and jeers I've enjoyed!

As a "rap," while snapping fingers:

> Data, data, data.
> Things were gettin' badda.
> Data, data, data
> Told us whatza matta.
> Data, data, data.
> Now it's goin' up the ladda.

As a cheer, with motions:

> Data, data, data's
> Just yadda, yadda, yadda (thumbs to fingers like lips flapping)
> Be a clown! (any funny pose)
> Turn it around! (twirl)
> Engage them all! (point around room)
> Have a ball! (arms form circle above head)

As a song to the tune of "Row, Row, Row Your Boat":

> C'lect, count, graph your data
> So you'll know your school.
> If you don't have proof to show
> You'll look like a fool.

As a poem dedicated to me:

> Does it really matta
> That we've gathered all this data?
> Our mission and duty we shall shirk
> If we don't put our data to work.
> The students may be smart or dumb
> Using data, we'll know Holcomb.[3]

Remember getting engaged? It was partly scary, but it was fun, wasn't it? So why shouldn't there be some fun getting engaged with data?

Notes

1. Bracey, G. (1997). *Understanding education statistics: It's easier (and more important) than you think.* Arlington, VA: Educational Research Service.

2. Sylwester, R. (1995). *A celebration of neurons: An educator's guide to the human brain.* Alexandria, VA: Association for Supervision and Curriculum Development.

3. This clever play on words was pronounced "how'l come" by poet Terry Balster of New Berlin, Wisconsin.

4

Arousing the Passion

The more things change, the more they stay the same. It used to go like this: "How many of your schools have a mission statement?" No hands. Now it goes like this: "How many of your schools have a mission statement?" Almost all the hands. "Who will tell us what your mission statement says?" No hands.

I'm puzzled. "If you don't know what it says, how do you know you have one?" The answers are usually,

"We did one in an inservice once."

"The Board went on a retreat and did one for the district."

"It's on the bottom of our letterhead."

Saying we have a mission statement but don't know what it says is like saying I'm a good driver but don't know what the speed limit is. I'm still going to be held accountable if I get pulled over.

If so many mission statements are lying around on letterheads without making a difference, why devote a chapter to it? Because a mission statement is one of the ways we can articulate the common core values of an organization, and it has the *potential* to make a radical difference. In his study *Peak Performers*, Charles Garfield noted the passion that some individuals have for their endeavor.[1] He described their sense of mission as "an image of a desired state of affairs that inspires action, determines behavior, and fuels motivation." That's how you know if your school really has a mission statement. Does it inspire action? Does it determine behavior? Does it fuel motivation?

In *Asking the Right Questions,* I described an affinity process for developing a mission statement that has been used by schools that don't have one or believe they need to try again.[2] In Chapter 1 of this book, I pointed out the need for alignment between our mission statement and our school portfolio—what we say we're all about and the evidence of what we really do. Colloquially, it's expressed as "putting our money where our mouth is."

The activities in this chapter are meant to engage people's passion so we'll want to deliver the proof. I believe that almost all teachers chose their careers based on a sense of mission. I also believe that at least an ember of that passion still smolders somewhere deep inside the most burned-out veteran in the profession. I've discovered, somewhat to my surprise, that getting engaged with data can help rekindle that passion. Here's one way.

Monitoring Our Mission

Some mission statements just float out there with nothing to grab on to. Some data just sit and stagnate because they don't seem to connect with anything meaningful. The simple form in Figure 4.1 can help people make those connections.

Before using this activity, verify that the school has a mission statement and have it ready on a transparency. If you are working with a group of people from various schools, have a sample mission statement participants can use for practice if they don't have one or can't remember it.

Ask the participants how many of them know they have a mission statement for their school or district.[3] Give them a few minutes to find it in something they brought or work together to write it down as accurately as they can recall it. Offer the example you brought for practice or show them the transparency of their own mission statement as an "answer key" to see how well they did.

Next, call attention to the first column of Figure 4.1. Our mission is what we say we will do as a school. It's a set of commitments. Ask the participants to look at their mission statement and circle the words or phrases that represent key components or commitments. Here's an example:

The mission of Our Town School is to provide a safe, orderly environment where students master their academic skills and become productive citizens and lifelong learners.

The key components of this mission statement are

- ◆ Safe, orderly environment
- ◆ Mastery of academic skills
- ◆ Productive citizens
- ◆ Lifelong learners

What We Say	Evidence We Have	Evidence We Need

Figure 4.1. Monitoring Our Mission

Have the participants write these words or phrases in the boxes in the first column because they are "What We Say" we will do.

Next, tell them you assume that considerable time and energy probably went into development of this mission statement and that there was strong support that Our Town School should accomplish these things. If so, we need to provide evidence that the mission is being fulfilled.

The second column is titled "Evidence We Have." The task now is to consider the types of data already available somewhere in the district and school that are relevant to that aspect of the mission. When I first began using this activity, I left it at that and was quite surprised at how "stuck" some groups would be. The lack of awareness of data that are regularly collected and probably communicated annually to all patrons is alarming. Now I keep a list of "Available Data" handy on a transparency and almost always discover it's needed to help groups get started (Figures 3.1 and 4.2 provide ideas).

As the participants identify indicators for the components of the mission statement, there will be comments like "We should be keeping track of that" or "We don't have any way of knowing" or "That can't be measured." These ideas go in the third column, where participants record types of data that will be needed. For example, many classroom teachers keep track of student behaviors that are related to employability skills, for example, tardiness, materials ready to work, and homework completion. This data may never have been compiled on a schoolwide basis, but it could be. We'll get to the "unmeasurables" later in this chapter.

After the groups have worked a while, ask them to take a look at the "Evidence We Have" column, and put an "S" by the items they've listed there that are student results and an "A" by those that are adult activities. The significance of the coding is to remind us that the evidence we need to produce is that something more or better is occurring for children. Traditionally, we have reported things like "We have DARE and peer mediation and conflict resolution" as evidence that we provide a safe, orderly environment. They are programs we offer—which is not the same as results we achieve. If the participants have listed types of data that are all adult activities, programs, and practices, encourage them to be sure that the "Evidence We Need" column will eventually provide indicators of results for students. (Chapter 5 describes how and where to include the adult activities in your school portfolio.)

The completed products fulfill several purposes. First, the process of filling out this form reconnects people to their mission statement. Sometimes it makes them decide to revise their mission or start over completely. Second, connections are made between the passion and the proof—what we believe is important to do and how we will know we're doing it. Third, the "Evidence We Have" column is the directory of items to include in the initial baseline version of the school portfolio (see Chapter 5). These types of data meet the criteria of being available and being of importance to the school. Fourth, the "Evidence We Need" column generates awareness of information that should be added as the school portfolio is continually updated.

The Unmentionable Unmeasurables

People I work with often say they've been told not to put anything in a mission statement or school improvement goal that isn't "measurable." So they shy away from things like character education and creativity. In the example above, productive citizen and lifelong learning might be considered unmeasurable if we think only of paper-and-pencil tests and numerical scores. But there *is* much more to what we accomplish as a school than just content and skills, and sometimes those are the things that inspire us most. If they arouse our passion, we should keep them in the language of our mission and goals. We just need to stretch our vocabulary from "measurable" to "observable." After all, we probably need to get more immediate data about lifelong learning than a postgraduation follow-up survey at the nursing home! Here's one way to approach it.

Challenge the participants to reflect silently and identify a person they know and regard as a lifelong learner. Ask them to jot down the things they see that person do or hear that person say that add up to their impression of lifelong learner. Then record a general list from the group. Prompt as needed to be sure the factors are all observable. For example, "He's a risk taker" needs the clarification of "What do you *see* him do that you call taking risks?" A typical list includes items like:

◆ Gets interested in something and wants to know more

◆ Goes to the library and gets books and gets on the Net

◆ Reads a lot

◆ Shares new ideas and knowledge

◆ Tries to get other people interested

◆ Takes courses and workshops that aren't required

◆ Likes to figure out his own way to do things

◆ Sets goals for himself

These are indicators of lifelong learning in an adult. We work with children to develop these characteristics. Now ask participants to link up with two or three others who teach (or parent) students of about the same age. Their task is to take this list and discuss, "What does each of these behaviors look like at age 17? at age 11? at age 7?"

Two observations usually emerge when groups report out. One is the conclusion that most of those behaviors look pretty much the same at any age and could be observed in the school setting. The second is a realization that many of the school's own practices limit the opportunity to observe these characteristics and may thus be inhibiting rather than nurturing their development.

Figure 4.2 provides an example of the Monitoring Our Mission activity completed for both the measurable academic skills and the observable characteristics of citizenship and lifelong learning.

Mission in Action or Missing in Action?

There is power in language. If not, we would be unmoved by Lincoln's Gettysburg Address or King's "I Have a Dream" speech. There is also power in the process of collectively articulating what is important, what is nonnegotiable, what is essential to our professional spirit. There is even greater power when the result of that collaborative product is actually used in daily life.

School improvement processes often recommend a structure that has a core leadership group in the middle, which spins off subcommittees to complete specific tasks. There may be a "mission committee" that coordinates the development of this important statement. Too often, it sees its work as done when it's hanging on the wall. Its work has only begun. Just as we need people who are by nature "number crunchers" to play a vital role in our work with data, we need people who are by nature "cheerleaders" and "zealots" to keep

What We Say	*Evidence We Have*	*Evidence We Need*
Safe, orderly environment	• discipline referrals • expulsion/suspensions • vandalism	
Mastery of academic skills	• scores on state assessments • percentage of students passing district criterion reference tests • Degrees of Reading Power test • ACT scores	• desktop access to individual student records of mastery • performance assessments (portfolios, exhibitions)
Productive citizens	• attendance/truancy • tardiness • homework completion • percentage of students in leadership roles (clubs, council, peer mediators, etc.) • number participating in co-op work experiences • graduation/dropout rate	• participation in community service activities (church, scouts, food drives, etc.)
Lifelong learners	• number and quality of independent projects completed • co/extracurricular participation • ACT participation • feedback from local business partners	• interview mature adults in community about what contributed to their lifelong learning habits • survey students about learning opportunities they pursue outside of school (piano, etc.)

Figure 4.2. Monitoring Our Mission—A Completed Example

our mission alive. Conscious planning should go into ways of referencing the mission frequently during faculty meetings and other events. Here are a few ideas I've learned from school "mission-aries:"

◆ When new staff members are hired, be sure that a presentation on the mission of the school is part of their orientation.

◆ When a tough decision is being made, ask the staff to complete statements like "This fits our mission because . . ." or "This doesn't fit our mission because . . ."

◆ Keep a Mission Box (version of Suggestion Box) in the office. Students, teachers, and parents can drop notes in it to report actions they have seen that exemplify the mission. Some of these can be read with the announcements or shared in newsletters.

◆ Short scenarios of problem situations can be presented to the staff. Ask small groups to prepare or role-play responses that are consistent with the mission statement.

◆ Have elementary students learn the vocabulary of the mission statement and draw what they think it means.

◆ Have students of all ages identify what their roles are in contributing to the mission of the school.

◆ While staff members are gathering for meetings, provide a mission-oriented quotation on the overhead projector, such as this one from Fullan and Hargreaves: "In collaborative cultures, the examination of values and purposes is not a one-time event . . . but a continuous process that pervades the whole school."[4]

Notes

1. Garfield, C. (1987). *Peak performers: The new heroes of American business.* New York: Avon.

2. Holcomb, E. L. (1996). *Asking the right questions: Tools and techniques for teamwork.* Thousand Oaks, CA: Corwin. See pages 41-45 for description of an affinity process used to develop mission statements.

3. The question of district mission statements and school mission statements arises occasionally. In my experience, district mission statements tend to include more components that address resources and facilities and long-range planning, whereas school mission statements can be more focused on teaching and learning and the school environment or climate. If there is a district mission statement that had lots of involvement and seems well accepted at the building level, that can work. If the district administration or board is adamant about only one mission for every school in the district, it concerns me, but there's no point in a school going through the time and effort to develop a mission statement if it can't use it to guide what it does. If the district mission is old or was developed without extensive involvement of teachers, then the principal may need to verify that it's permissible to have a separate school mission "as long as it does not contradict" the district mission. This is usually acceptable at the district level and poses no problem at the building level because our value systems are not that different.

4. Fullan, M., & Hargreaves, A. (1991). *What's worth fighting for in your school.* Toronto, Canada: Ontario Public School Teachers' Federation. Quotation is from p. 49.

5

So What's Significant?

A colleague of mine from the University of Wisconsin used the expression, "Schools are data rich and information poor." What he meant was that there are all kinds of data available in school districts, but very little is actually used to *inform* people and their decisions and actions. Those who worry about "where will we get any data" are forgetting—or aren't aware of—the multitude of grants, projects, and other funding sources that all have strings attached in the form of reporting requirements. Public schools also have accountability to state departments of education, who usually receive their mandates from federal and state legislatures, all of whom demand information on a frequent basis. The problem is that almost no one has a complete picture of all the data in a system, and who has it, and how to get it. The development of a school data collection is the first step of converting existing data into meaningful information. This chapter offers three ways to select data to be included in a school portfolio.[1] The *constructivist approach* uses critical questions to guide dialogue, the *compliance approach* responds to external demands for specific kinds of information, and the *minimalist approach* starts with whatever is at hand for immediate attention.

The Constructivist Approach

There are more technical definitions, but they vary from author to author, so I'll describe what constructivism is to me. It's simply *constructing* meaning

1. What evidence would demonstrate that we are fulfilling the commitments embedded in our mission statement?
2. Do we have any existing, ongoing goals that lack baseline data from which to measure progress?
3. Is there more than one source of evidence for this decision or more than one indicator of need for this goal?
4. What are the assumptions we make about students and their learning? What do we need to do to verify them?
5. What data might help resolve smoldering issues in our school?

Figure 5.1. Key Questions for Meaningful Data Selection

from facts, patterns, and other stimuli as compared to being told what things mean and what I should think about them. Rich dialogue around the following questions is one way to help staff, students, and constituents focus on data that would be significant to them—data they consider relevant, important, and helpful.

1. What evidence would demonstrate that we are fulfilling the commitments embedded in our mission statement?

The "Monitoring Our Mission" activity in Chapter 4 was a constructivist learning activity in the sense that it resulted in greater meaning attached to both the mission statement and the types of data that would show progress or accomplishment.

2. Do we have any existing, ongoing goals that lack baseline data from which to measure progress?

In Chapter 1, we discussed the importance of identifying improvement goals based on data. That's the ideal and should apply to any future goal set-ting. The reality is that I encounter few schools that can actually start their school improvement process with a clean slate. Most schools have something they are already working on, whether it was determined at the school level or imposed through some other process such as a district strategic plan or a state initiative. Whether existing goals came from internal or external sources, most were developed solely on the basis of participants' perceptions. Working on the initial school portfolio provides an opportunity to backtrack and decide what evidence is needed to establish a baseline from which to measure prog-ress.

On the day of this writing, a workshop participant showed me a goal aimed at parent participation in conferences. She said, "You know, we were frustrated because we feel we don't get enough support from parents. But I'll bet if we checked how many report cards had to be mailed home, we would discover that most parents do come to conferences. What we really want is something beyond that. So we need to check the data. If it's low, we should keep the goal. If it's not, we need more discussion of what we're really after. And maybe we should include parents in the discussion." Right!

3. Is there more than one source of evidence for this decision or more than one indicator of need for this goal?

This question applies both to existing goals like the parent conference example and to pending decisions and future goals. A basic principle from research is the concept or term *triangulation*. Long before global positioning satellites, the term described navigation at sea using charts, instruments, and a few bright stars to plot current location and direction. Its application to decision making for school improvement is the need it implies to have multiple indicators that confirm where we are and where we should be going.

In discussing Question 2 above, I implied reservations about goals set "solely" on the basis of participants' perceptions. That is not to say that perceptual data is not important. It is. But it is usually not sufficient. Perception that is confirmed by objective indicators is far more valid for decision making. In the absence of "hard" data, perceptions that are shared by more than one group provide a better basis for action. Here are examples of both kinds of triangulation as support data for school improvement goals.

Elementary School A's goal is, "All students will increase their application of math computation, concept, and problem-solving skills in all curricular areas." Here are three indicators—two objective and one subjective—of the need to address student achievement in math:

◆ Standardized test scores below the state average for math problem solving

◆ Only 60% of the students mastering the district's math outcomes based on locally developed criterion-referenced tests

◆ Former students of Elementary School A who have completed sixth grade at Middle School B stated in focus groups that they were not prepared for the challenges of math at that level.

High School C's goal is, "All students will increase their application of computer skills across the curriculum." Support data presented for this goal include:

◆ Student survey results requesting more chances to use computers

◆ The SCANS report emphasizing computer literacy as an essential employability skill

◆ Community interest expressed through a $1.2-million referendum for technology

All of these indicators could be referred to as subjective or opinion, but in combination they provide a powerful case for this goal. Certainly the community has spoken through the ballot box, and the school must respond with a clear focus and comprehensive plan to use these resources well and provide evidence that the taxpayers' money was well spent and is making a difference for students.

4. What are the assumptions we make about students and their learning? What do we need to do to verify them?

The increased emphasis on high-stakes accountability mentioned in Chapter 2 has also escalated the amount of "blaming the victim" I observe in school conversations. "Our test scores would be better if they didn't make us test learning disabled kids." Or, "We'd be doing fine if we only had to count 'our own' students and not the ones who are moving in and out all the time." These comments provide clues to factors that should be used to disaggregate test data. Disaggregated data helps us separate the "whys" from the "whines."

Disaggregation is *dis*mantling the *aggregate* information that is typically reported to us as a mean or average number. These measures of central tendency are relatively useless for understanding our students. Bracey states this concept as a law: "No measure of central tendency without a measure of variation."[2] After all, how many "mean" students do you have in your school? Returning to data that is "raw" enough to show us range and distribution will help us understand the patterns of success and failure in our student population much better. We must always be asking, "Does this tell us about our whole school? Or about which kids? Who are we seeing reflected here? Who are we missing? Who may be falling through the cracks because we've rolled them all up into one big average?"

Demystifying Disaggregation. If the term or concept of disaggregation is unfamiliar to your group, try one of these two quick illustrations. Because I am "vertically challenged," I ask the audience to identify two other people who are about 5 feet tall to stand with me. Then I ask for three volunteers to stand who would describe themselves as 6 feet tall. Looking at six people like this, ask the group what their mean height is. Then pause and ask, "And how many of them are 5 feet 6 inches tall?" Continue by asking what would be the easiest way to increase the mean height of the group standing. The answer is to send a short person home. The discussion can be further pursued by pretending that we are going to select a basketball team. What assumptions might we make? Yes, take the tallest. What else might we need to know? Yes, who can shoot. Disaggregating data about student achievement is like analyzing the field goal and free throw percentages of all the students to check our assumptions about height and basketball ability.

Another example that works well uses weight, so don't ask for volunteers for this one! Tell the group to imagine that you weighed each person as he or she entered the room, calculated the mean, and posted a sign on the door that says, "The average weight of people in this room is 195 pounds." What would passersby think about that information? Would they know if it was good news or bad news? Would they think this is a weight loss group or a steroid users support group? After some humorous speculation, people will indicate that it depends on other information about the group, such as how many of each gender, age, and height. When we report information on student learning as a mean, it tells us about as much as the weight sign on the door.

Figure 5.2 provides a response to the earlier comment about including students with learning disabilities in the state assessment testing. Instead of a single number representing the mean, this stacked bar graph shows the percentage of students achieving in each quartile. In a normal distribution, 25% of the students would score in each quartile. In Figure 5.2, the scores of Exceptional Educational Needs (EEN) students have been disaggregated and the distribution of scores without them is compared to the distribution of achievement for the total school population. Even when Special Education students were included, 75% of the 4th graders, 79% of the 8th graders, and nearly 83% of the 10th graders scored above the 50th percentile. Teachers in the district were amazed at how similar the two bars looked when the scores of EEN students were removed from the results for the overall population at each grade level.

Figure 5.3 shows how a school disaggregated data to test assumptions about increased mobility in the district. This simple 2 × 2 grid was constructed based on criteria the school chose. When asked to identify a "cut score" that would determine adequate achievement, the school chose the 40th percentile because of its link to Chapter 1 funding. (This was before the 1994 reauthorization that returned to the Title 1 nomenclature.) The school was also asked how long a student would have to be in the district before it would accept responsibility for the student's learning. The school chose 2 years. The perception that the mobile students were failing at a far greater rate than the stable population had to be abandoned in the face of data to the contrary.

Does this mean that teachers' perceptions about students are always false? Of course not. Sometimes our worst fears are confirmed. But the willingness to question our assumptions is a major step away from the conscious and unconscious ways we convey low expectations for some students and a major step toward building a collaborative culture in a school. When our assumptions are confirmed, we have valuable information that will help us select the most effective strategies to use with a targeted population.

The Bottom Fourth. Sometimes our assumption is that there *are* no subgroups in our student population because it appears so homogeneous. There are no obvious racial differences, and socioeconomic status seems fairly level, with most of the students' parents engaged in the same few occupations with similar incomes. In these situations, preselecting a variable as the basis for disaggregation may seem like an exercise in futility. The alternative is to identify the bottom fourth of the students on any important measure. For example, look at grade distributions and select the bottom fourth of the students. Or

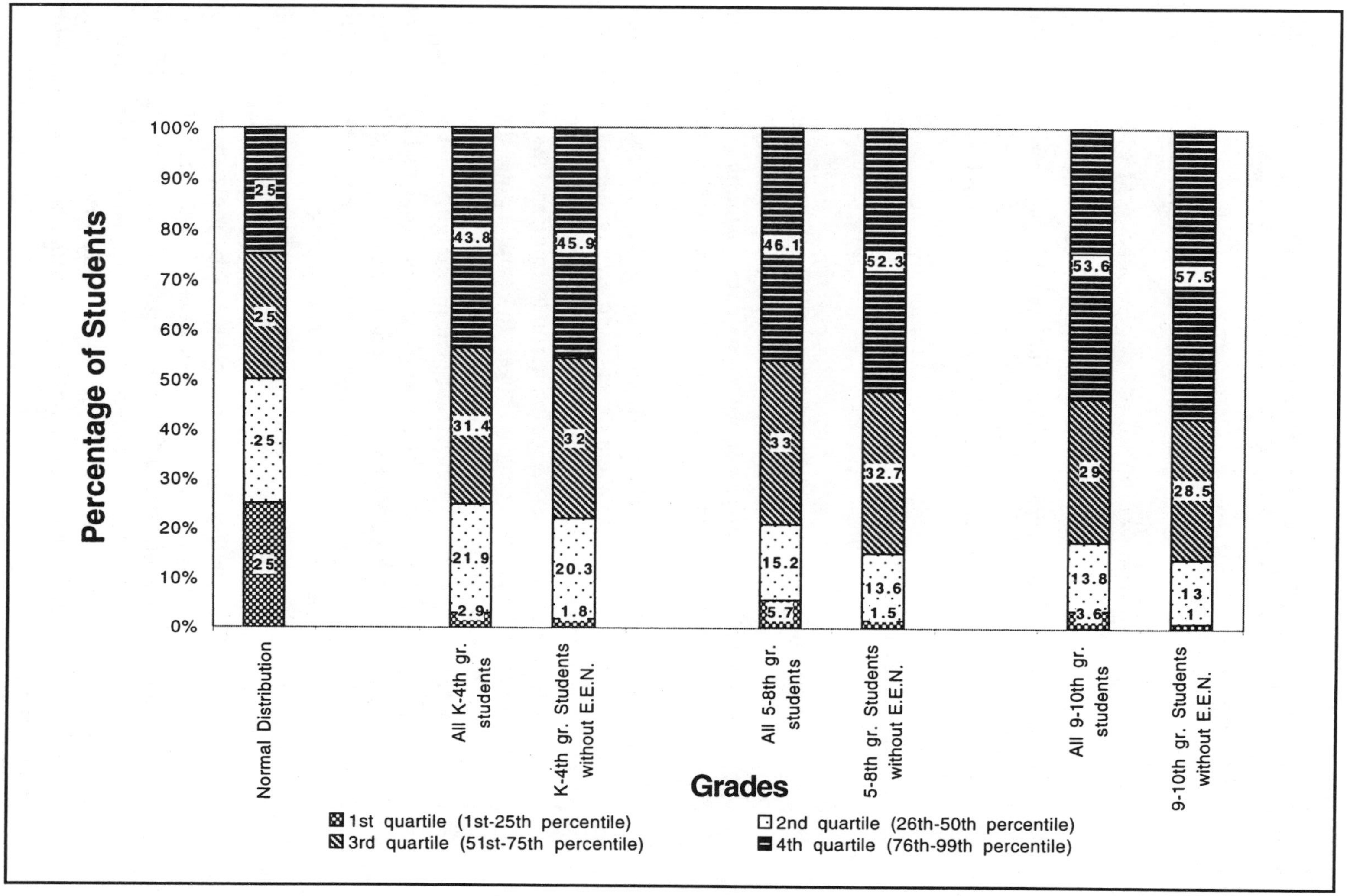

Figure 5.2. Scores on State Math Assessment—Distribution by Quartile With and Without Scores of Students With Exceptional Educational Needs (EEN)

	In district less than 2 years	*In district 2 years or more*
40th percentile or above	93% (n = 28)	92% (n = 72)
39th percentile or below	7% (n = 2)	8% (n = 6)

Figure 5.3. Reading Achievement Scores Disaggregated by Mobility

look at attendance and select 25% of the students with the most days absent. Discuss these students by name and see if they have any common characteristics that may have been overlooked in the assumption of homogeneity.

5. What data might help resolve smoldering issues in our school?

Many schools are plagued by conflicts that just won't go away because people are divided into camps based on philosophy or preference. The development of a school portfolio can be a window of opportunity to gather data that may resolve these dilemmas or, at least, create better understanding of the situation.

At School D, the issue of open or closed campus had been bantered about for months. Arguments raged about rights of students versus risks of driving, nutritious lunch menus versus drive-through junk food, and supervision versus duty-free noons. The question of impact on learning had never surfaced. When the school improvement team began to compile data, the members asked themselves whether there was any information that could shed light on this issue. That's when attendance data became meaningful—not as an aggregated percentage of all students for the whole year but analyzed by period of the day. Figure 5.4 shows the pattern of student absences the team discovered. Based on this data, the staff voted for closed campus. By serendipity, the staff also noted the increased absences during last hour and began to explore possible explanations, including scheduling of study halls and implications of student employment.

At Brooklyn Elementary School in Brooklyn, Wisconsin, frustration was high among the staff because the lunch personnel seemed to take too long to serve the children and this reduced their lunch time. The teachers thought the answer was more kitchen staff to serve the children. Based on the menus, teachers predicted how long it would take to complete serving. The staff then monitored the lunch line for 10 days to verify the actual time it took students to be served. Each teacher recorded arrival time, time the first student was served, and time the last child was served. Figure 5.5 shows that the effects were much less than teachers expected. On 8 of 10 days, the variation in serving time for the whole school was 4 minutes or less. On every one of the 10

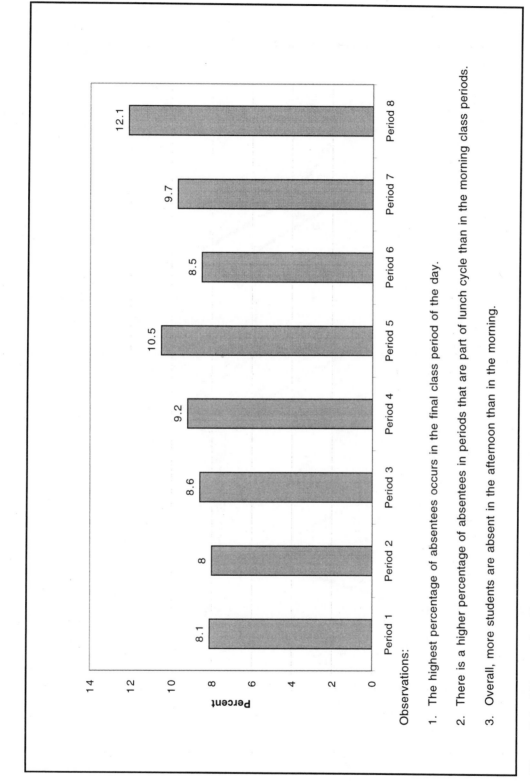

Observations:

1. The highest percentage of absentees occurs in the final class period of the day.

2. There is a higher percentage of absentees in periods that are part of lunch cycle than in the morning class periods.

3. Overall, more students are absent in the afternoon than in the morning.

Figure 5.4. Absences by Class Period—Grading Period 3

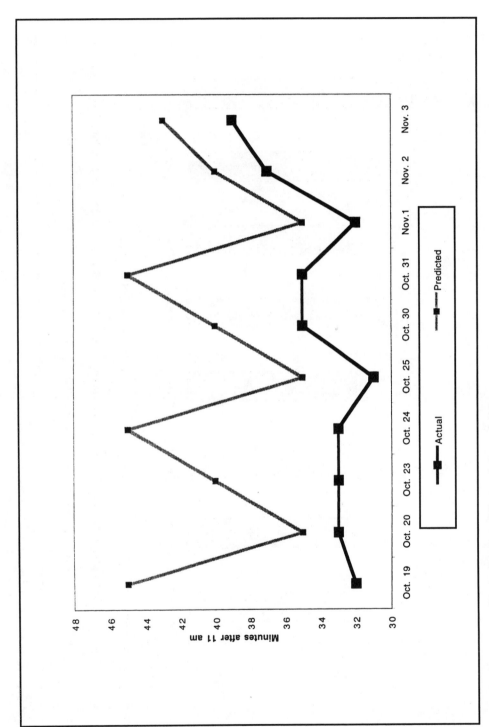

Figure 5.5. Time of Last Student Through Lunch Line

days monitored, the actual serving time was from 2 to 12 minutes less than predicted. Ruffled feathers were smoothed, and time and energy that might have been expended on a staffing issue could be conserved for other purposes. This type of data, gathered to resolve a specific problem, might be included in the school portfolio or might simply be compiled and analyzed to better understand a situation.

The Compliance Approach

Given the almost universal reluctance to tackle data, I'm always surprised when a school group says, "Just tell us what you think we should put in our school portfolio and we'll get it together." This assembling of data in response to a set of external requirements is what I call the compliance approach. Such guidelines are available from a variety of sources, including accreditation organizations, recognition programs, and state mandates.

The NCA Way

The North Central Association of Colleges and Schools (NCA) requires schools to develop a profile as part of its accreditation and endorsement processes.[3] Five categories of data are needed:

◆ Unique local insights

◆ Follow-up of former students

◆ Data on student characteristics

◆ Instructional data

◆ Community data

Community needs assessments and climate surveys are used to provide insights on the unique nature of the local context for schooling. Information on former students includes typical graduate follow-up studies, focus groups and interviews with students who have moved from elementary to middle school or middle school to high school, and feedback from dropouts. Sometimes feedback from universities and employers can also be obtained.

Typical data on students include enrollment, attendance, suspensions and expulsions, dropout rate, standardized test scores, ACT and SAT participation and scores, mobility, and cocurricular participation. These data are disaggregated to compare performance of various groups within the student population.

Schools seem to have more difficulty compiling instructional data, and usually include staff development participation and surveys of most common instructional techniques. This is the appropriate place for information about what the school provides in the ways of programs and opportunities. The adult activities that were listed during the "Monitoring Our Mission" activity in Chapter 4 can provide data for this section.

Community data may include a description of local, state, and federal mandates that affect the school or demographic information on population trends, income, and employment.

Blue Ribbon Criteria

The U. S. Department of Education's recognition program has been known as National Schools of Excellence and Blue Ribbon Schools. I have been honored to participate in this process in various capacities since 1991 and have seen its increasing emphasis on assessment and documentation of results in student learning. Complete answers to questions in the 1997 nomination form for high schools required these kinds of data:

Demographic Data

◆ Enrollment by grade level

◆ Per pupil expenditure

◆ Racial/ethnic composition

◆ Student mobility rate

◆ Percentage of limited English proficient students

◆ Percentage of students qualifying for free or reduced-price lunches

◆ Percentage of students receiving special education services

Student Data

◆ Student participation rates in nonacademic services and programs

◆ Student participation in cocurricular activities and the degree to which it is representative of the overall composition of the student body

◆ Percentage of students who exceed graduation requirements

Data on Teaching and Learning

◆ Usage data from library, information, and media services

◆ Number of students moving among ability groups, especially into groups with more challenging course work

◆ Participation in professional development and evidence of impact on improved teaching

◆ Evidence of how analysis of data at the school level has resulted in specific improvements

◆ Evidence of how technology has contributed to increased use of data for decision making

Data on School, Family, and Community Partnerships

◆ Data on family involvement in school activities and the degree to which the families involved are representative of the overall student body

Indicators of Success

◆ Results of standardized tests for each of the last 5 years, disaggregated according to the largest and most significant subgroups in the school
◆ Results of nonstandardized, or alternative, assessments developed at the school level
◆ Results of college entrance examinations (PSAT, SAT, ACT) and percentage of students tested
◆ Percentages of students in various educational and employment categories a year following graduation
◆ Daily student attendance
◆ Student dropout rate
◆ Daily teacher attendance
◆ Teacher turnover rate
◆ Results of climate surveys
◆ Percentages of students involved in various types of safety, discipline, and drug issues

Through the data included in the nomination form, schools must demonstrate that student outcome results are consistently outstanding or that significant improvement has been achieved during the past 5 years.

State Dictates

Like most state education agencies, Wisconsin's Department of Public Instruction collects indicators of quality that are required by state law to be reported to the community each year. These include

◆ Scores on Wisconsin Reading Comprehension Test (Grade 3)
◆ Scores on Wisconsin Student Assessment System—Knowledge and Concepts examinations (Grades 4, 8, and 10)
◆ ACT results
◆ Advanced Placement testing
◆ Advanced course work
◆ Graduation requirements
◆ Graduation rates
◆ Postgraduation follow-up information

◆ Extracurricular and/or cocurricular activities

◆ Attendance

◆ Out-of-school suspensions

◆ Expulsions

◆ Retentions

◆ Dropouts

◆ Habitual truants

◆ Staffing ratios

◆ Revenues and expenditures

This list can be a starting point. It certainly identifies data available in every district. But there are several important distinctions between a state performance report like this and a school portfolio. The most obvious one is the difference between a mandated list and a collection of data chosen by the school as having significance for it. A second is that states are interested in district information and the school portfolio is focused on the individual building. If a district is large enough to have more than one school at any level (elementary, middle, high school), the district's data will need to be broken down by building.

The third difference is that state reports are primarily quantitative, whereas school portfolios should include a balance of quantitative and qualitative data to reflect perceptions of staff, students, and constituents. Perhaps the most important contrast is the type of comparisons made. State reports are used to compare districts throughout the state. A school portfolio would include two different types of comparisons. One is comparison of the school's own performance over time (see Chapter 6). The other would be comparisons to schools that are similar in nature and achieve desired results. This is *benchmarking*, as the term is used in the business sector. A business asks, "Who's in the same kind of business we are with the same kind of product trying to reach the same market—and doing it best?" A school might ask, "Who works with a similar student population in a similar context and has high achievement?" These comparisons help identify models for further study and can lead to networking with other schools.

Constructivist Compliance

An advantage of the compliance approach is that it is more efficient. The data are readily available and the work plan is fairly clear. A disadvantage is that it's more difficult to create ownership and interest. When schools are required to report certain types of data in a certain way or in certain categories, I encourage them to start with a few of the key questions from Figure 5.1 to get people engaged and then "slide" the data that's of intrinsic interest under the headings required by their state or district model.

The Minimalist Approach

There are times when it's most appropriate to apply the K-I-S-S principle to the school portfolio. That's "*Keep It Simple and Succinct.*" This might be necessary if timelines for goal setting are growing short and it's important to have at least *some* data to use as a first step toward more data-driven planning. It may also be prudent if there is a high level of resistance or if a new form of data requires a lot of time and energy. The first year schools that received results from high-stakes statewide assessments may be such an example. In East Troy, Wisconsin, the curriculum coordinator took this simple approach. Dr. Sara Larsen distributed copies of the reports from the state assessment to small groups of teachers and asked them to identify what type of reports would be most useful to them as they evaluated their curriculum and teaching strategies. Of course, it didn't stay minimalist for long. By the time they listed the ways they would like the data analyzed, the teachers had also requested information of most of the types already listed in this chapter. But at least they *started* small.

The key to getting people engaged with data is *start somewhere.* The "somewhere" is wherever they are now in terms of readiness.

Notes

1. Whenever I use the words *select* or *selective* in relationship to the school portfolio, I am referring to size, not bias. The school portfolio shouldn't be a public relations product that reports only the good news, nor should it be a deficiency document of only the concerns. It should be accurate but not create information overload in addition to all the other challenges of work with data.

2. Bracey, G. (1997). *Understanding education statistics: It's easier (and more important) than you think.* Arlington, VA: Educational Research Service. Quotation is from p. 7.

3. North Central Association Commission on Schools. (1997). *Developing the school profile: A handbook for schools.* Tempe, AZ: North Central Association of Colleges and Schools.

6

It Matters How It Looks

Chapter 5 described approaches to *selecting* data that will be considered meaningful, relevant, and useful to a school's staff, students, and constituents. This chapter focuses on *displaying* the data so it is clear, accurate, and user friendly. How the data looks does matter. Realtors use the term "curb appeal," referring to the first impression that clients have as they approach and drive by a property. A house could have a beautiful interior and an attractive price, but if it's not visually appealing, the sale will be difficult. In the same sense, if a school portfolio isn't visually appealing, the task of engaging people in discussion of the data and its implications for planning and decision making will be that much more difficult.

Size

A first consideration is size. In Chapter 5, we stressed the need to be selective about how much of all the available data to compile in a document that will be reviewed and discussed by all. Many principals I work with have at least one 4-inch three-ring binder of data about their school and students. It's available to anyone who wants to review it. They also have the mini-version: a small 1/2-inch binder or packet of data that is used for discussion purposes. Guidelines from the North Central Association of Colleges and Schools recommend a collection of about 20 pages, with only one or two data displays per page.[1]

User-Friendly Data Displays

The second consideration is how to display the data. Figure 6.1 illustrates three major parts of a data display: the introduction or explanation, the graph, and the summary statements or findings. The title is clear and long enough to let the reader know whether this is the information being sought.

The Introduction

A short paragraph should be included to explain what test was used, who and how many were tested, when the test was given, and how it was analyzed. Since this is an illustrative example, the name of a specific test is not given. Schools should name the actual test and the form or level that is administered. This paragraph should spell out any acronyms used on the page and define terminology, such as *socioeconomic status* (SES) and *percentile*. This is an important lesson I learned the hard way—through an embarrassing discussion with a community member who had misread SES as SEX and proceeded from there to an irate protest against gathering data on who's high, middle, and low in that function.

The Graph

Each axis should be clearly labeled, and any unfamiliar terminology should be explained in the paragraph at the top. If scores are in percentiles, the % sign should not be used. Percentiles should be shown as simply the number, with the word percentile along the side. Or the "ile" suffix should be added to the number (79 %ile) or the number should be printed as 79th, or 63rd, or 82nd. This is an important distinction, because many readers who see 79% will believe that students answered 79% of the items correctly. A few years ago I attended a community forum of school board candidates in which a candidate stated, "The district's test scores are in the 70s and when I was in school, 70s meant a D. Our schools are only performing at the D level."

It's also important to be careful about how the range is shown, especially on the vertical axis. If the data is in percentiles, the full range from 0 to 100 should be shown. If the school's scores are all below the 70th percentile, the graph should not be cut off at the 70th just to save space, because readers may say the axis only went up to 70th to make the scores look higher than they really are.

In *Asking the Right Questions,* Chapter 3 was devoted to data that helps answer the "Where are we now?" question. Pages 15 to 32 provide suggestions and examples of the use of histograms, pie charts, run charts, and pareto charts as ways of displaying data.[2]

Beware of the "color trap." With newer software and color printers, it's quite simple to create beautiful multicolored graphs. These are eye appealing and easy to read—if you have an original copy. But school portfolios are frequently copied for reference or distribution. If you are going to use color, be

All students in grades 2-5 take the standardized test every October. These are the results for this year's students in each grade. Qualification for free or reduced price lunches is used to identify students as having lower socioeconomic status (SES). The percentile rank indicates that our students scored higher than such a percentage of students taking the test nationwide.

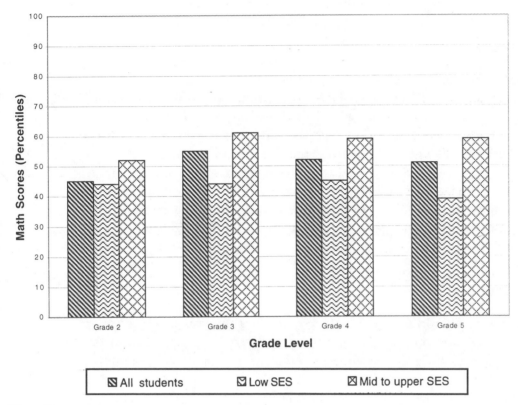

Strengths:
1. The means of math scores for all students in grades 3, 4 and 5 are above the 50th percentile.
2. The mean math scores for middle and upper SES students are above the 50th percentile at all grade levels.

Concerns:
1. The mean for all 2nd grade students is below the 50th percentile.
2. At all grade levels, lower SES students score below middle and upper SES students. The discrepancy ranges from 7 percentiles on the second grade test to 20 percentiles on the 5th grade test.
3. It appears from this data that lower SES students fall further behind in math as they progress through the grades.

Figure 6.1. Scores on Standardized Test of Elementary Math Disaggregated by Socioeconomic Status (SES)

sure that you also have a color copier or are willing to print multiple copies directly from the computer. Otherwise, stick to various patterns of black and white so the codes used for bars, lines, and segments of a pie chart aren't lost in reproduction.

The Summary

Figure 6.1 summarizes the data with two statements of strength and three statements of concern. The next chapter describes a professional development activity that engages teachers as the interpreters of data, so this section would not be developed by an individual or small group charged with constructing the graphs. It would be added later based on the interpretations done by staff. These statements must be factual observations, not evaluative judgments. For example, we state that the mean for all second-grade students is below the 50th percentile. We do not say that second graders have the poorest performance or that we must improve performance of second graders. The latter would be a rush to judgment on what should be the school's improvement goal. Chapter 8 provides further cautions about premature goal setting.

Some schools prefer to write one paragraph or make one general set of summary statements rather than separate strengths from concerns as in Figure 6.1. This is a local decision. It may be less threatening to avoid the headings, but the disadvantage is that items needing improvement are easier to ignore and the thrill of celebrating successes is often missed as well. The choice of "Concerns" as a heading, rather than using "Weaknesses" as the antonym of "Strengths," is very deliberate.

A Self-Test

When the school portfolio—or each individual data display—is considered finished, two self-tests should be imposed. The first is to ask one or more persons who are not involved in any way to look at it and see what questions they raise or if they are able to answer a few key questions you ask about it. The second is to "fold the page in half" and see if each half can stand alone. In other words, would a person who is strongly visual or spatial and may look only at the graph get exactly the same message that a person who is strongly verbal or linguistic would get from reading the narrative only?

Displaying Longitudinal Data

The purpose of this book is to engage schools in greater use of data as a step toward the essential mission of schools, which includes improving student performance. Chapters 5 and 6 focus on selecting the data to be gathered and displayed as baseline information in an initial school portfolio. But the school portfolio is a *continuous work in process*. (Take another look at the shaded arrows in Figure 1.2.) Your school portfolio will be updated at least once a year as another round of test scores are received and another state report is submitted. For the school to see evidence of improvement, data must also be displayed over time. Figure 5.5 showed a run chart, or line graph, of lunch line times during a 10-day experimental period. I have seen line graphs used in many other ways, but it's technically correct to use a line graph only if the line represents the same variable over several points in time.

Different Students. A series of bar graphs can be constructed so that they compare performance of different students at the same point in their schooling. Figure 6.2 presents 4 years of math scores from Templeton Middle School in Sussex, Wisconsin. This improvement over time was accomplished simply by placing emphasis on the test as an important event in the school year. Teachers explained why the test was important and how the results would be used to help determine their individual goals for seventh and eighth grade. Students were given the practice test from the publisher, and announcements to parents emphasized attendance, proper rest, and encouragement for the students to do their best but not worry about the outcomes.

The data in Figure 6.2 are from 4 years of sixth-grade students, so it's true that each bar represents a different set of students. This is often a hang-up for teachers, especially those who survived statistics courses designed to prepare experimental design researchers rather than to equip practitioners for responsible decision making. It *is* sound practice to use data from different groups of students to reflect on the role of the school and engage in program improvement. Unless the size of the school and the group tested is very small, or there have been major demographic changes in the student population in a short period of time, student performance will remain relatively stable when compared to a nationally normed, random population. When the population is reasonably stable and the reference point is a large national sample, the school can infer that improvements are due to its efforts. The small "s" on efforts is critical. In our daily life in schools, we do not have a laboratory where cause-and-effect relationships between one specific strategy or invention can be isolated and "proven" or where a matched control group and experimental group can be identified. That's why Chapters 9 and 10 refer to multiple strategies and assessments. We will never know what specific step we took on a given day with a specific student that improved learning. We *can* see student scores improving and know that the holistic effect, the synergy of our combined efforts, does indeed elevate the overall performance of our students.

The Same Students. In some situations, perhaps for you, this is not a good enough answer. Longitudinal data can be gathered for the same cohort of students as they move through their schooling in a district, but it takes time and money that most of us don't have. The same tests would have to be administered every year, and the scores of every student who was not in the initial group removed from the analysis. This assumes that the district has complete control over its assessment program, which is not true in most states. In Wisconsin, the 4-year history of state assessment includes two different test companies, three forms or levels of the test, and a shift from fall to spring testing.

I know of two approaches that schools are using to account for changes in assessment programs. Bob Armstrong, research consultant for the North Central Association of Colleges and Schools, recommends use of a formula to convert all scores into standard (z) scores. This requires statistical computations at the local level.[3]

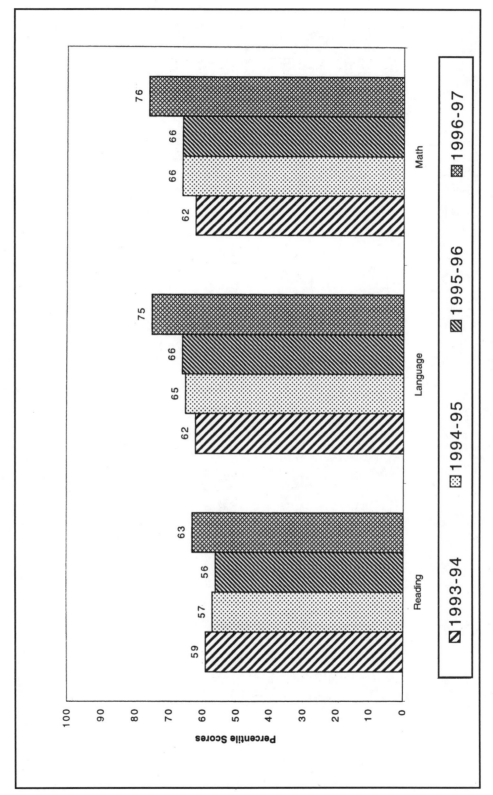

Figure 6.2. California Achievement Test Scores for Sixth Grade, 1994-1997

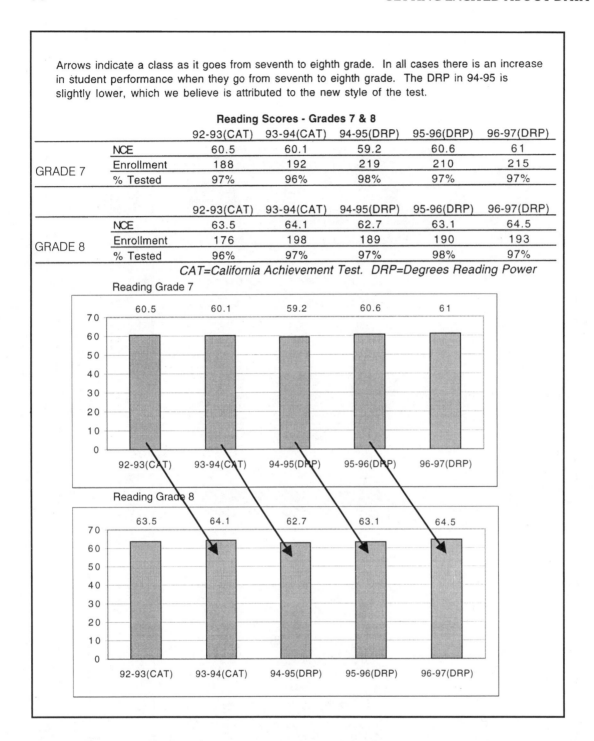

Arrows indicate a class as it goes from seventh to eighth grade. In all cases there is an increase in student performance when they go from seventh to eighth grade. The DRP in 94-95 is slightly lower, which we believe is attributed to the new style of the test.

Reading Scores - Grades 7 & 8

		92-93(CAT)	93-94(CAT)	94-95(DRP)	95-96(DRP)	96-97(DRP)
GRADE 7	NCE	60.5	60.1	59.2	60.6	61
	Enrollment	188	192	219	210	215
	% Tested	97%	96%	98%	97%	97%

		92-93(CAT)	93-94(CAT)	94-95(DRP)	95-96(DRP)	96-97(DRP)
GRADE 8	NCE	63.5	64.1	62.7	63.1	64.5
	Enrollment	176	198	189	190	193
	% Tested	96%	97%	97%	98%	97%

CAT=California Achievement Test. DRP=Degrees Reading Power

Reading Grade 7

Reading Grade 8

Figure 6.3. M. T. Bailey Middle School California Achievement Test, 1992-1994, and Degrees of Reading Power Test, 1994-1997 (in Normal Curve Equivalents)

A more convenient method is the use of normal curve equivalents (NCE).[4] Figure 6.3 is an example from the U.S. Department of Education's Blue Ribbon Schools nomination packet. It illustrates the use of NCEs to compensate for a change from use of the California Achievement Test (CAT) to the Degrees of Reading Power test. Since most test companies include NCEs in their reports, this does not require use of a conversion formula.

Displaying Perceptual Data

One of my difficult, time-consuming tasks has been responding to "If we send you our school portfolio, will you take a look at it and let us know if we are on the right track?" I always agree to do so, because these are busy people with the courage to tackle a new challenge, and I want to reinforce their efforts and help them avoid setbacks. It's a delicate task, though, because it's hard to know how much feedback they can really handle all at once. One suggestion I always make is, "Don't report survey data by listing all the survey items and all the responses with a number or percentage next to them." This may go on page after page, and no reader is going to invest as much time as I spend looking for which items have the highest and lowest levels of agreement and satisfaction. (If the raw data goes on page after page, the survey was probably too long to start with.) Then there may be even more pages that list every comment made in response to open-ended questions. I suggest that all of this data belongs in the principal's 4-inch binder, but only a synopsis belongs in the school portfolio for discussion. Perceptual data can be displayed as graphs, as seen in Figures 6.4 and 6.5.

Figure 6.4 is a pareto chart that shows the percentage of students in an elementary school who answered yes to a short yes-or-no survey of 17 items. What makes it a pareto chart is that the items are organized from the one receiving the strongest affirmation, "Grownups at school care about me," to the item receiving the least affirmation, "I have time to eat lunch." This arrangement makes it easy to condense survey data and readily identifies the items of least satisfaction that may need to be addressed.

Figure 6.5 illustrates a way to display perceptual data from various role groups. In this example, a survey of 25 items included 5 items that related to each of 5 categories: Feelings of Safety, Focus on Teaching and Learning, Individual Help for Students, Fair Rules Consistently Enforced, and Home-School Communication. The detail of responses by item would be available for those interested in an in-depth look. What the data display can capture is a sense of which group is most pleased with which aspect of the school, and where there is highest and lowest agreement between the responding groups.

Listing all the responses to open-ended questions can be problematic in several ways. The first is the natural tendency of human beings to try to figure out who said what. The second is that satisfied patrons seem not to have much to say, whereas dissatisfied patrons, who may be in a distinct minority, may generate a great deal of verbiage. To keep such responses in perspective, I

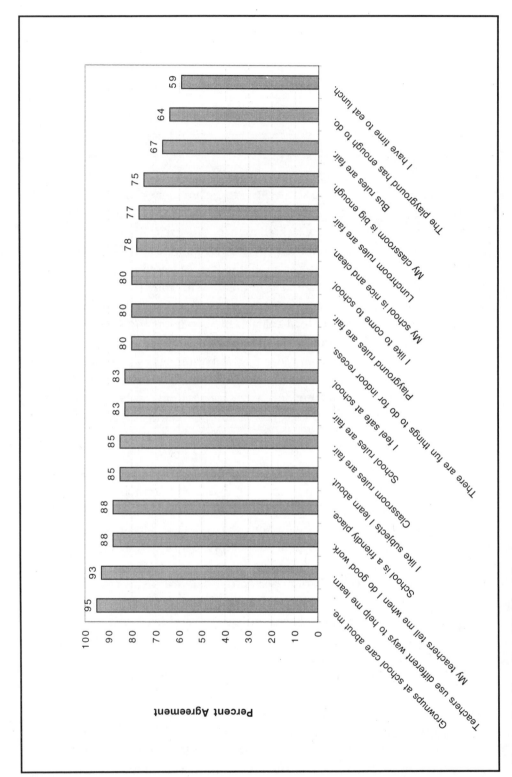

Figure 6.4. Results of Student Survey

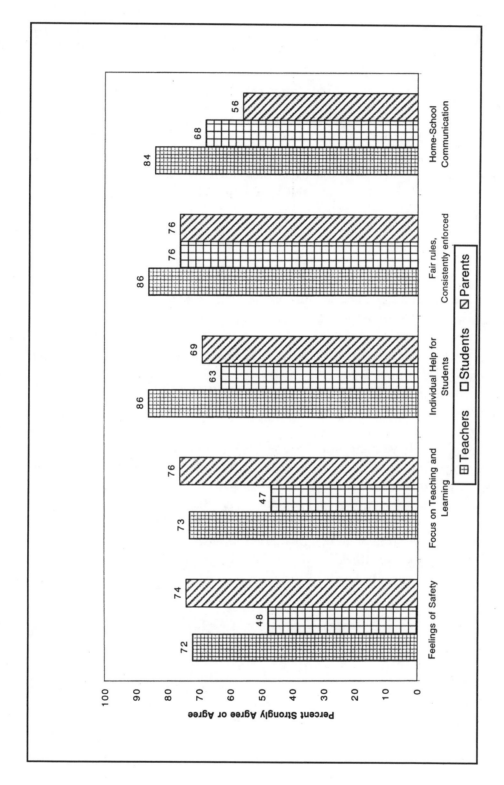

Figure 6.5. Survey Responses From Teachers, Students, and Parents (mean of 5 items per category)

recommend that each survey received be given a code number, and that code number be noted after each comment as it is listed. It is then possible to differentiate between "22 negative comments" and "22 negative comments from 2 respondents."

The Acid Test

Let's assume that at this point your school has 15 pages of data. On each page, there is just the introductory section and a graph. Chapter 7 suggests a way to empower your staff by engaging all of them in interpreting the data. The acid test is this: Do your data displays look like something your teachers can understand—or will at least discuss—if it's a nice, warm afternoon and they've been teaching all week?

Notes

1. North Central Association Commission on Schools. (1997). *Developing the school profile: A handbook for schools.* Tempe, AZ: North Central Association of Colleges and Schools.

2. Holcomb, E. L. (1996). *Asking the right questions: Tools and techniques for teamwork.* Thousand Oaks, CA: Corwin.

3. Armstrong, R. (1998, March). *Presenting the evidence.* Paper presented at the 103rd Annual Meeting of the North Central Association of Colleges and Schools, Chicago.

4. Since I have cited Gerald Bracey (1997) twice in support of my content, it is only fair to share his opinion of NCEs: "Avoid them unless the feds force you to use them" (*Understanding education statistics: It's easier (and more important) than you think.* Arlington, VA: Educational Research Service. Quotation is from p. 31). My position is that the normal curve equivalent is an *available* alternative to what may be the greater evil of neglecting to examine our students' progress over time.

7

Figuring Out What It Means

$\mathcal{S}$pring break had come and gone, and the countdown was under way. It wasn't the last day of school we were anticipating. It was the release of the test scores. Principals and teachers knew they had arrived in the district, because the corner window of the Research and Evaluation Department was lit up until the wee hours for two straight nights. It meant that the test expert was poring through the printouts, preparing them for dissemination to the buildings.

When we received them a few days later, we knew what mattered. The areas of student performance that would have been stated as concerns in Chapter 6 were highlighted on each report. A memo was attached directing us to study them carefully and respond within 2 weeks with an improvement plan. It wasn't motivating and it didn't increase interest in working with data for several reasons:

- ◆ The implication was that staff at the school were not willing or capable to identify areas of concern for ourselves.

- ◆ The absence of acknowledgment that our students did very well in some areas created resentment and added to the emotional barriers described in Chapter 3.

- ◆ The expectation that a 2-week window during the last month of school was either adequate time or the appropriate time to develop a sound improvement plan was ludicrous.

Preparing the Materials

◆ Enlarged copies of the data displays

◆ Questions for discussion on flip chart paper

◆ Colored markers

◆ Post the data displays and questions at stations around a large room with blank wall space

Preparing the Participants

◆ Structure groups of 5 to 11 that cross department or grade-level boundaries

◆ Have groups designate a facilitator and recorder

◆ Colored marker travels with the recorder

Questions for Reflection

◆ What do these data seem to tell us?

◆ What do they not tell us? What else would we need to know?

◆ What needs for school improvement might arise from these data?

Figure 7.1. Carousel Data Analysis

My ground rule for interpreting data is, "Let them do it themselves." My message to teachers is, "Let's do unto the data before the data gets done unto you." Figure 7.1 outlines the structure of a staff development activity that engages staff in discussion, empowers them to interpret what it means, and allows them to express reservations about its use.

Preparing the Materials

Two factors to consider in preparation are space and time. The room to be used should be a large room with plenty of blank wall space for posting graphs and questions. This is one professional development activity that *does* work fine in a lunchroom or gym. People can "think on their feet" and move about, which is an important way to release tension if this is an unfamiliar task.

Time is related to the amount of data ready for staff review and the number of staff members who will be participating. A general guideline is that this activity takes 1 1/2 to 2 hours. That would accommodate a staff of 50 with 15 data displays to consider. They would be divided into 15 groups of three to four in each group. There would be 15 stations to visit. At 5 minutes per station, the data review would take 75 minutes. Similar arithmetic will help you plan your time and groups.

Variations can be made for a group of 100. One is to have groups of seven or eight people. Another is to have two sets of graphs and operate two sets of stations. A third is to have larger groups and cluster several related data displays at each station.

Preparing the Participants

Groups should be structured before the event to help cross the natural boundaries of grade level or department that people naturally drift into. This structuring can be done in a straightforward manner such as by posting the rosters. Or a lighthearted approach can be used, with methods such as putting colored dots on name tags or numbers on the sticks of lollipops or base of ice cream cones.

Take the first 15 minutes to explain the purpose of the activity and the reasons the participants have been placed in groups. The purpose is to give everyone an opportunity to view all the data that's been prepared for the school portfolio. The participants are being asked to contribute to the interpretation of the data and provide input to complete the data displays. The groups are a way of encouraging new discussions with people they may not see often and sharing various perspectives. Their activity is modeling the collaborative culture that looks at the "big picture" of the whole school (rather than how the department is doing) and experiencing a sense of the collective responsibility that a school staff should share.

The numbers or color codes of the groups will help participants find the other members of their group and the station where they will start. Give them a few minutes to get located and to choose the facilitator and recorder for each group. The group will have a designated time at that station. The task is to discuss the data that is shown and react to each of the questions. The recorder will write members' reactions on the flip chart paper that is posted. After the designated time, at a signal announced in advance, each group will move to the next station to review another type of data.

The kinesthetic value of moving from station to station was already mentioned. Another benefit is that each group reviews the reactions of other staff members, increasing the shared perceptions in another way. An alternative is to have groups seated at tables and provide each table with a set of all the data displays for discussion. The same input may be provided, but the interaction of the groups with each other and the awareness of what other groups have said is missing.

Questions for Reflection

The questions for reflection and discussion have been carefully worded. The first question does not say, "What do these data tell us?" but "What do these data seem (or appear) to tell us?" People will see different things in the same data, and someone is sure to quote Mark Twain's comment, "There are lies, damn lies, and statistics." Words like *seem* or *appear* acknowledge that the conclusions may not be cut and dried.

The second question provides further acknowledgment that a single snapshot of data may not tell the whole story of what we need to know to make decisions. Asking, "What else would we need to know?" sends a clear message that these are not the only data we will ever see.

The third question raises awareness of the fact that these data will guide goal setting, decision making, and planning in the future. Including the word *might* reminds us that these are tentative conclusions at this point.

Figure 7.2 is a graph of cumulative grade point averages that was posted at one station of the Carousel Data Analysis at Templeton Middle School in Sussex, Wisconsin. The interpretations recorded by staff members are listed in Figure 7.3. The principal, Patricia Polczynski, reports, "The experience of gathering information, putting it in graph form, and then allowing the staff to 'pick it apart' and determine what it means to us has been eye opening and powerful."

A five-question version of the Carousel Data Analysis was proposed by one of the districts in the Goals 2000 Consortium. The questions were:

1. What do these data seem to tell us?

2. What do they not tell us?

3. What else would we need to know?

4. What good news is here for us to celebrate?

5. What needs for school improvement might arise from these data?

The addition of the fourth question provides an opportunity to highlight successes and may alleviate some of the frustration described in the scenario at the beginning of this chapter.

The Results

The responses to each of my three questions have a specific use as the school moves forward with its school improvement process. Responses to the first question will be synthesized to form the summary statements at the bottom of each page of the school portfolio. Input on what else we need to know will guide further data collection as the school portfolio is reviewed and refined each year. These ideas will also be useful when the school begins to select strategies to increase student achievement. Chapter 9 describes the need to further analyze areas of concern before making decisions about change. Chapter 8 utilizes answers to the third question as a tentative list of improvement areas that will be reviewed in preparation for goal setting.

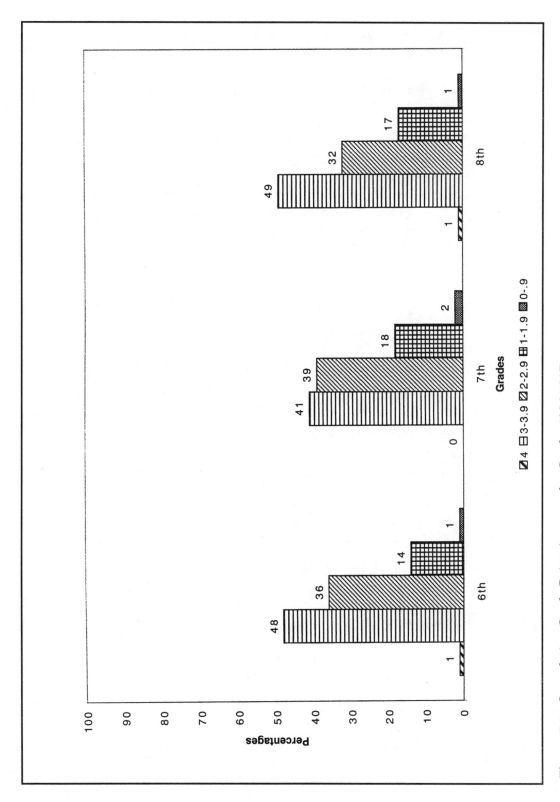

Figure 7.2. Cumulative Grade Point Averages by Grade, 1996-1997

1. What does this graph seem to tell us?
   80% of the students in each grade are average or above.
   The plateau of 7th-grade brain growth correlates with this graph.
   There is a very high percentage in the 3.0 to 3.9 range.
   Small percentage of low GPA.
   Majority fall within 3.0 to 3.9 range.
   70% fall at or above "C" level.
   40% or better are 3.0 to 3.9 for all Grades 6, 7, and 8.
   Only 1% are at 4.0 or better.
   30% to 40% or better are 2.0 to 2.9.
   8th grade has highest with "B" averages—81%.
   7th grade has highest failure rate:
   ◆ lowest percentage of "B" or above and no one with 4.0 GPA
   ◆ more "clumped" with 80% achieving 2.0 or higher
   No drastic differences in grade levels overall.
   Decline a bit in 7th grade.
   Percentages are close.
   7th-grade achievement is relatively lower in all grade points except
      for 2.0 to 2.9; it also has the highest number of students with the
      lowest grade point average.
   At least 40% of each grade level has a cumulative GPA between 3.0
      and 3.9.
   Less than 20% of each grade have a cumulative GPA between 1.0 and
      1.9.
   7th grade has the lowest percentage of high GPAs.

2. What does it NOT tell us?
   Academic ability of students
   Specific information as far as courses (allied v. academic), teachers,
      etc.
   Group dynamics of each grade
   What they actually know versus grades
   Teacher expectations/grading expectations
   Attendance information
   Gender differences
   Doesn't reflect grade scales by teacher or grade
   Doesn't reflect weight of time frames (some classes are ¼ as long, etc.)
   7th and 8th can choose electives
   Motivation, effort, parent support

3. What other information would be needed to make this graph more
   useful?
   How our students compare to other districts in terms of breakdown
      per grade level
   Follow the same age throughout their stay at this school
   What individual teachers' expectations are for A, B, C grades

Figure 7.3. Carousel Data Analysis of Cumulative Grade Point Averages

8

People, Passion, and Proof in Goal Setting

Depending on whose research you read, school reform either takes 3 to 5 years or 5 to 7 years. One reason it takes so long is that the school improvement process isn't the only thing going on in a school. That's why it's critical that change efforts focus on a few goals that are systemic and substantive enough to motivate sustained attention and impact student learning. This chapter describes a process through which students, staff, and constituents can generate all their concerns and then participate in identifying priorities and sharpening this focus. We will then address how to phrase goals so they keep the focus on student learning and point out the danger of confusing goals with strategies.

Getting It Out and Narrowing It Down

The goal-setting process I have used for the past several years is a combination of the traditional nominal group process and the use of a decision matrix. These two techniques are described separately in *Asking the Right Questions*.[1] What I've discovered is that the nominal group process can result in agreement on goals derived solely from the opinions of the group. If reference to data about the school's and students' performance is lacking, people end up wondering why they went to all the trouble of compiling the school portfolio.

Without baseline data, schools also end up with no basis for comparison to show progress. Use of the decision matrix brings both objective and subjective data to the table. As Doris Thompson, principal of Lake Mills (Wisconsin) Middle School said, "Teachers do think about students' needs when they plan, but they will like being able to verify that by looking at the real evidence."

The steps in this hybrid process are

- ◆ Review of the data
- ◆ Individual reflection
- ◆ Round-robin listing
- ◆ Individual rating on three criteria
- ◆ Adding individual ratings
- ◆ Individual ranking of five priorities
- ◆ Group ranking of five priorities
- ◆ Discussion
- ◆ Repetition of individual ratings and rankings as needed

Note how many steps occur before discussion. This sequence was developed to provide an opportunity for participants to share all concerns, engage in personal reflection, and observe how their ratings compare to the rest of the group before becoming verbal.

Review of the Data

In the previous chapter, we discussed a "carousel" activity in which participants moved in groups from station to station, discussing compiled data and responding to three critical questions. The third question asked was, "What needs for school improvement might arise from these data?" The kickoff for this process is to review those responses. It is certainly appropriate to have the list typed and provide copies for the participants, but sometimes a more powerful connection occurs if the actual flip chart sheets from the earlier activity are saved and displayed again.

Individual Reflection

After participants have a chance to review the tentative concerns previously identified, stimulate further reflection by posing a question like, "What are all the things that anyone might say could be improved about our school?" As the question is displayed, underline the word *all* and emphasize that this is the participants' opportunity to create a comprehensive list for consideration. They should be candid and jot down any concern they have on scratch paper provided.

Then call attention to the word *anyone* and remind them to present not only their own viewpoints but viewpoints of others they are aware of from survey data or private discussions. Stress that the word *could* expresses our commitment to continuous improvement and does not imply that the current situation is so awful. We're simply expressing our openness to look closely at all aspects of our school.

Observe the individual reflection and allow time until most participants seem to be done writing. Emphasize that every one of their concerns will be included and that it will be helpful if they look them over to be sure they are specific and easily understood. Suggest that longer statements be reduced to a short three- to five-word phrase. Omitting verbs from the list of concerns keeps the focus on the issues rather than what action should be taken.

Mention that a concern like "student test scores" will be more helpful if it is broken down into specifics like "reading achievement" or "math problem solving." Even if that makes the lists longer, it is good to subdivide such general items, because reading scores and math scores would be approached differently if they became the school's goals.

Round-Robin Listing

If the group consists of 25 or fewer participants, serve as recorder and conduct the round-robin listing yourself. If you are working with a large group, divide it into smaller units and have each group select a recorder. Group members designated as recorders can give their concerns to another participant who will be sure that the items are included.

Round-robin listing means that each person states one concern from his or her list, and this is repeated around the circle. Emphasize that everyone must listen carefully and cross off items that other people mention to avoid duplication and keep the process moving quickly. The recorder should assign a letter to each item as it's listed to facilitate ranking and discussion later. In addition to the public recording, each participant should jot down the items on the form you have provided (Figure 8.1). Unless participants create their own lists as you go, use of the decision matrix will be complicated and confusing.

If you have facilitated a small group, you now have one list of all members' concerns. If you divided a large group into smaller groups that actually represented different schools, each group has its own total list and will rate and rank those items. But if everyone in a large group is from the same school, take a break and combine the separate group lists into a total master list. This can be done quickly during a break for the large group, either by repeating the round-robin exercise on flip charts or by word-processing all the responses and then printing the master list for each participant. (If you plan to do this, participants will not need to write in the concerns on Figure 8.1.)

Individual Rating on Three Criteria

I've learned through study and experience that people get more motivated to work toward goals if there is clear evidence of need, an intrinsic sense of their importance, and a feeling that the goals are achievable and within their

AREA OF CONCERN	HOW SEVERE? Rate each item 1-5. 5 = greatest dissatisfaction with results, i.e., lowest test scores, worst problem, etc.	HOW CRUCIAL? Rate each item 1-5. 5 = most important issue; needing most immediate attention; most essential to the mission.	HOW RESPONSIVE? Rate each item 1-5. 5 = most amendable to change; within power of school.	TOTAL OF INDIVIDUAL RATINGS	INDIVIDUAL RANKING Rank order 5 items only with 5 as highest priority.	GROUP RANKING

Figure 8.1. Goal-Setting Matrix

reach. The three criteria of the decision matrix reflect these characteristics of "goals that get done." Ask participants to deal with one column at a time so you can clarify the directions and keep the group in about the same place.

The first question, "How severe?", provides one more opportunity to connect with the data. Participants give ratings of "5" to any concerns they feel are severe, especially areas of student performance with the lowest test scores or survey items with high percentages of dissatisfaction. Remind participants that they can give the same rating—whether 5, 4, 3, 2, or 1—to as many items as they wish.

The second question, "How crucial?", emphasizes the need to establish goals that are closely linked to the mission of the school or are particularly urgent and important. Urge participants to ignore the ratings they gave in the first column and rate each item according to this criterion only.

The third question, "How responsive?", allows participants to acknowledge that some concerns may be severe and crucial but outside the scope of influence of the school. Use of this column addresses reality and feasibility. Ratings of "5" are given to those concerns that the school can address most independently. A rating of "1" indicates that the participant feels the school really can't do anything about it.

Adding Individual Ratings

The column labeled "Total of Individual Ratings" is provided so participants can add the three ratings they gave to each item. Point out that an ideal goal would have a total of 15, because that would identify a severe need that is crucial to the effectiveness of the school and that the school can address. True 15s are rare. The principle is that the higher the total, the more priority the item deserves.

Individual Ranking of Five Priorities

Based on the individual ratings, each participant is to choose his or her top five priorities. A helpful tip is to provide stick-on notes and have the participants put the letter code of each of their top five priorities on one note. If a group member is most concerned about items labeled A, E, J, M, and P, there would now be a slip of paper with a letter A, another with E, a third with J, and so forth. The participants can move the stick-on notes around in case they want to change their priorities but should end up with a 5 on the same card as their top priority, a 4 on their next, and so forth. Double-check to be sure all have 5 for their top priority. (Usually someone does this ranking backward.)

Group Ranking of Priorities

When participants have ranked their items, ask them to alphabetize their stick-on notes to speed up the group ranking. As you call out a letter, go quickly around the circle and have each person who ranked it state the numerical value he or she gave it. Write down each ranking rather than just add them mentally and record a total. When discussion takes place, it will make a difference whether one concern has a total value of 20 because 10 people ranked it a 2 or because 4 people ranked it a 5.

After all concerns have been tallied, total the numbers. In most cases, there will be a group of concerns that cluster together with high scores and then a drop down to another set or the rest of the list.

Discussion

Now is the opportunity for discussion. Set a few ground rules, which may include the expectation that only advocacy statements will be made. This means that people express why they think a concern is of great importance and should be one of the top priorities for goal setting, but that speeches against specific items are not appropriate. Sometimes it's also necessary to set the number of times that any individual can speak or the length of time for any individual comment.

Repetition of Ratings and Rankings

In some cases, a second round of rating and ranking is unnecessary because the priorities become very clear and the discussion does not indicate strong disagreement with any of them. If there is disagreement or if questions are raised about some items, ask if those who "gave it a 5" would share their reasons for being so concerned about it. Sometimes their responses will provide new information for other participants and cause them to shift their priorities. On other occasions, questions will raise the need for more accurate information before a final decision is reached. In this situation, help the group decide what information is needed, who can provide it, and what time will be needed to get the information. Then schedule another meeting to look at the information before a second round of ranking determines the school's priorities. The process should continue until two to five priorities have been determined.

Variations for Participation

All interested parties should be invited to participate in the goal-setting process, but it may not be feasible to do it all at once because of group size and scheduling considerations. The process can be broken into phases, and multiple groups can participate and have their input added. For example, staff might generate their list of concerns during a faculty meeting, students might contribute theirs during homerooms or in a representative fashion through a student council meeting, and parents might engage in the round-robin listing at a PTA meeting. If these three events are held in the same week, Figure 8.1

can be prepared as a synthesis of the concerns raised by all three groups. The items could even be coded as to origin. For example, "SSP" might mean that staff, students, and parents all generated this concern. Each group could meet again the next week and do the ratings and rankings, which would then be combined, and so forth.

Participants who come to a goal-setting session expecting arguments and tension are relieved to see that there is a safety net in the form of a structured but inclusive process. Jeanne Anderson of Jim Falls Elementary School in Chippewa Falls, Wisconsin, put it this way: "I have done many kinds of goal setting and this is the best. It's slick and easy but very sound. It takes the stress out of this important step in school planning."

How We Say It Does Matter

Once the few priorities for improvement are identified, the next engagement is to develop a goal statement for each one. Although I resist and resent consultants and administrators who take a "fill in the blanks" approach to mission statements and goals that need to be intrinsically powerful, I do have some observations about wording goal statements. Here are two examples I use to generate discussion. I ask groups to comment on differences between the two statements.

◆ To increase computer access and develop an integrated technology curriculum

◆ All students will increase their application of computer skills across the curriculum

Participants observe that the first one doesn't mention students. It's a statement of what the teachers and district will do. The bottom one says what the children will do. Is it possible to do the first goal without students being affected at all? Sure. The district could buy more computers and hire teachers to write curriculum during the summer and report to the board that the goal was accomplished—with no impact on students at all.

The second statement is systemic enough to drive change in a whole school. Fulfilling it would involve acquiring hardware and software; dealing with facilities and location for access; and identifying the computer applications students should be able to use, how they would be integrated into each discipline, and what products would be created. Staff would also have to develop performance assessments that students would do to demonstrate the computer skills and determine when students could do them. Would they be assessed in classes or sign up at a computer lab to test out?

The emphasis of this book is on the use of data. Once goals are set, it should be possible to look backward and forward from the "Priority Goals" spaces on Figure 1.1 and see the data connections.

◆ Do the improvement goals accurately reflect data that were reviewed? Is there evidence to support the need for this goal as a priority to sustain several years of effort?

◆ Will the evidence that demonstrates achievement of the goal be evidence of what more students can do more of, do better, do differently?

Most schools have issues that need to be addressed that don't relate to student performance. It may be more accurate to say these are issues that relate to learning *in*directly, because it's hard to imagine anything occurring in a school that would be of concern to a large number of staff, students, and constituents and yet be so isolated it would have no connection to learning or the learning environment. These issues can be handled as additional goals or may be considered as strategies to help meet a goal. On a few occasions, I have had to stop after the round-robin listing and address the fact that many items on the list would not qualify as student-centered improvement goals. I point this out before the individual ratings are done and ask which items we could code with an "s" because they are actually strategies. We set these items aside and save them for consideration later in the planning process.

An example that could be an additional goal is relations between staff and administration. If this is a major concern, it certainly affects the teaching-learning environment and needs to be addressed. I would call it an additional goal to emphasize that it is not a substitute for goals aimed directly at improving student performance.

Parent involvement is an example of a concern that might become a strategy in service of one of the student learning goals. If there is a goal that relates to improving students' reading achievement, part of the planning may involve how to engage parents specifically in helping their children with reading. Or if there is a goal that aims to increase students' responsibility for their learning and behavior, parents could be involved in developing strategies to help parents teach and reinforce students for taking responsibility.

The End or the Means

In the goal-setting process, we suggested that noun phrases without verbs be used to express the area of concern. This is because verbs are action words and imply what action should be taken. The actions are the "Strategies" section on Figure 1.1, and a lot of things should occur in the previous box, marked "Study." When people become committed to a strategy rather than a goal, the focus becomes fuzzy.

One day I received a call to meet with members of the leadership team of an urban elementary school. An out-of-state consultant had returned their school improvement plan, criticizing their goals. They didn't understand the feedback, and I was nearby and free, so they asked me to help them sort this out. These are the goals they had:

◆ To set up a writing-to-read computer lab

◆ To use the Degrees of Reading Power test

◆ To implement James Comer's school development/mental health model

I began by asking team members to describe their school and their students and how they reached these goals. Then I asked them to be patient as I probed with "why" questions. Why do you want to set up a writing-to-read lab? Because IBM will give us the computers. Why is it worth the trouble of writing the grant to get the computers and find a place for them and get them set up? Because then the kids can use them. Why do you want the kids to use them? Because there's research that shows that the computer makes it easier and more exciting to write, and when they write more they learn to read better or faster. So what is it you really want? For students to read better. Ah ha! The goal is that students improve their reading performance. The computer lab is a strategy. It's one of the means. It's not the end in and of itself.

Next we tackled the Degrees of Reading Power test. Why do you want to use the Degrees of Reading Power test? Because the standardized test we give now just has subtests of phonics and alphabetizing and discrete skills like that, but it doesn't really tell us if they can *read*. Why do you like the Degrees of Reading Power test? Because it has real passages for students to read and gives us a better measure of comprehension. Bingo! The goal is that students increase their ability to read and comprehend. The Degrees of Reading Power test is one of the assessments (see Figure 1.1) that will be used to monitor accomplishment.

Similar discussion about Comer's mental health model revealed that the school had a diverse racial and ethnic population and team members worried about low self-esteem and lack of pride among the students. They wanted to get social service agencies and churches involved with the school to build self-esteem and pride in the students. The model was the strategy, not the goal. To keep our school improvement plans aligned, we must be clear about *what* we want to accomplish, before we identify *how* to achieve it.

Note

1. Holcomb, E. L. (1996). *Asking the right questions: Tools and techniques for teamwork.* Thousand Oaks, CA: Corwin.

9

Digging Deeper

We ended Chapter 8 with a clarification of the difference between goals and strategies and a caution about leaping to strategies without sufficient study. The old adage "Haste makes waste" applies very well. Time, money, and energy can be wasted if we rush to implement new programs or practices that don't match our students' needs or our school culture or don't have any prior evidence of success in accomplishing goals like ours. It's not only our time that may be wasted. Each year that goes by without effective intervention is a year that our students move on and out of our classrooms and schools. Figure 1.1 includes a "Study" box with three bullets, which represent further analysis of the issue or need, investigation of research and best practice, and determination of appropriate ways to assess accomplishment of the goal.

Further Analysis of the Issue or Need

For strategies to be effective, they need to match the need and our situation. When my car was out of alignment, I could have purchased the very best tires on the market, but if they didn't fit they would only make the problems worse. The fish bone, or cause-and-effect diagram, and Garmston's "Go for the Green" activity are two ways to help people dig deeper and develop a better understanding of the issue. Both techniques are described in *Asking the Right Questions*.[1] This chapter repeats a classic example from my previous book and adds a new one for your consideration.

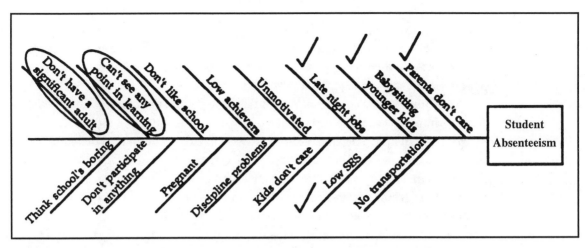

Figure 9.1. Cause-and-Effect Diagram of Student Absenteeism

Cause-and-Effect Diagram

A cause-and-effect diagram is a visual representation of the relationship between contributing factors and an issue or problem. Because the picture branches out like the skeleton of a fish, it has become known as a "fish bone."

The question, "What factors contribute to . . . " is stated across the top and the "head" of the fish represents the need or issue being analyzed. A horizontal line represents the spine of the fish. Some formal group process handbooks emphasize that causal factors fall into categories and that the categories should be identified first and the first "fish bones" should represent these categories. For example, quality management fish bones often start with the four categories of procedures, people, policies, and plant. I have left the process unstructured because I've seen too many groups get stuck figuring out what the categories might be. I'd rather have them dive into the discussion and attach smaller "bones" and "barbs" as they identify items that relate to each other.

After the diagram is drawn, guide the group to analyze the factors participants identified. Acknowledge factors over which the school or organization has no control. Then focus in on the factors that most closely match their perceptions of their own situation and that they are able to influence and willing to address. These become their "entry points" and will guide their selection of strategies or interventions.

The example used here comes from one of the most powerful transformations I have observed as a consultant. It not only demonstrates how to do the activity; it also answers the question, "Won't all this emphasis on data make us less humane and forget about students' feelings?"

Ten school leadership teams had been selected to participate in a 3-day workshop that would guide them through the process of developing a school improvement plan. They had been asked to bring student data and draft versions of any work they had already done on mission statements, goals, or action plans. It was fascinating to observe their approach to the day.

At one table sat a group of newspapers. It would have looked like a display at a newsstand, except that every now and then a hand would reach out and feel around for a coffee cup, which would then disappear behind the newspaper—more specifically, the sports section.

At another table, a group of early arrivals were poring over a stack of computer printouts. Heads together and unaware of the caterer's late delivery of the pastries, the participants were engrossed in a discussion of which subtests from a recent assessment matched their curriculum and mission closely enough to merit major attention as they set their improvement targets.

Another group entered carrying the lid of a copy paper box with waves of green-and-white striped computer paper spilling haphazardly over the edge. Locating the table with the school's name on it, the carrier dropped the box onto the floor—*thud!* and kicked it under the table with the side of his foot—*thwack!* Having thus dispatched the dreaded data, this group attacked the coffee and doughnuts table with much greater zeal. One member asked in a stage whisper, "So what's with this woman we have to listen to about effective schools? Somebody report us as being *de*fective or what?"

I was beginning to have qualms about the day, when another member of that group approached me and began a speech. "In all fairness, I really ought to let you know that there's no reason for us to be wasting 3 days at this workshop. We already have our school improvement plan done." Swallowing hard, I asked him what they had planned for the coming year. "Well, we got our biggest problem figured out. It's kids not coming to school. And we've got two plans for working on it. First, we got a business partner that's going to donate us some equipment so we can program it to call those kids and get them going in the morning. Second, we got a committee all lined up to work on our attendance policy so these kids can't get by with skipping. And we'd rather spend our time working on that than sitting in here."

I managed to thank him for his honesty and ask him to stick around for this first day, listen carefully, and think about his school's plan, and at the end of the day we'd talk again and see what could be worked out to honor his group's time. "Well, I guess we might as well. We're already here and, besides, it's raining."

During the first part of the morning, I engaged the group in a review of research on school effectiveness and provided an overview of the activities we would be doing over the 3-day period. I gave each group some time to talk about whatever data they had available and share the concerns that emerged from this discussion or others that had taken place at their school. During the report out, members of this group repeated that their attendance data showed a need for improvement.

Lunch was provided in the room right next door—and it was still raining—so we continued into the afternoon. That's when we began to discuss the importance of understanding the problem we're addressing and some of the causes or related factors so we know where to begin changing it.

The group began its fish bone of student absenteeism with "Parents don't care" and went right on to list items like "No transportation," "Baby-sitting younger kids," "Pretty low socioeconomic," and "Stay up too late at their night jobs." The other groups were getting along well, so I tried to coach this team a little. "You seem to have a pretty good handle on the students' family situation. Got any thoughts about the kids themselves?"

The next phase began with "Kids don't care either," "Unmotivated" (when they hold down night jobs?) and went on to "Discipline problems," "Low achievers," and "A couple of them are pregnant." About this time, I noticed one person sort of digging around under the table, but it had a skirt around it and I didn't want to get too nosy, so I ignored him.

The work on the fish bone was bogging down again. I tried sympathy. "It's really too bad some kids are like that, but I'm glad to see you're aware of them. Could there be any other source of factors that relates to whether kids come to school or not?" A soft voice from the other end of the table said, "Well, they don't like school when they do come." Several people just stared at her, so I reached over with my own marker and wrote, "Don't like school" on a new fish bone. A few others added things like "Don't participate in anything," "Can't see the point of learning," and "Don't seem connected to anyone."

Just then, a head popped up with the copy paper box in his hand and a dazzling grin on his face. "Wait a minute. I've just been digging through here and it looks to me like there's no more than 20 kids in the whole school that are causing our attendance rate to look so bad." My challenger responded immediately. "Oh, yeah? So, who?"

As the analyst mentioned a name or two, other members of the group began to comment on individuals. "Well, if Joey can just make it from the bus to the door without a fight, he does pretty well in class." "Sam doesn't have any trouble getting here, but he's so interested in messing around the art room he doesn't follow his schedule." "If Suzy wasn't so worried about her weight, she might have time to think about her work."

Because of the data, the participants suddenly began to talk about students as individuals. As they did, one brave soul said, "You know, if they are so low socioeconomic, do you think they'll have phones to call?" Another drew courage and said, "If they really don't care about school, what good will it do to suspend them for skipping?" My challenger shrugged and said, "Well, maybe our plan isn't quite right, but look at that fishy thing. We can't do anything about that stuff."

I delightedly agreed. "You're right. There are a lot of things that are beyond our control. Let's mark them off and see what we have left that we could tackle." Check marks on Figure 9.1 shows the items they eliminated. But they didn't check off very many because some members of the group began to argue that maybe the system *could* make some kind of provision for transportation and that they had heard of some schools that provided in-school child care. As the last step with their fish bone, they circled the items that could be entry points for a new action plan.

The next morning this group got there first. By the end of the day, the group had developed a plan that would provide each of the chronic absentees with an adult in the school (teacher, custodian, volunteer) who would check in with him or her each morning before school and follow up at the end of the day to see if the student was taking work home. The mentoring plan the group created is included in Chapter 10. A year later I met an administrator from that district at a conference and asked how things were doing. He told me that this particular school had made the most progress with its school improvement plan and that it was changing the culture of the school.

Go for the Green

Bob Garmston introduced an activity he called "Go for the Green" at a workshop called "Premier Presentation Skills," which I attended several years ago. It is one of the most valuable techniques I have found to help groups deal with subjective data. It can develop greater empathy and minimize "blaming the victim." You will need large chart paper, and black, green, and red markers.

Start with a red circle in the middle of the paper. Let the participants know that you are using that color deliberately, because this is the target. It reminds us of a stop sign because it prevents accomplishment of their task or goal. Maybe it angers them so they "see red." Help the group decide how to phrase the concern and write it in red. The example shared in Figure 9.2 is from a group that had been discussing student disengagement and lack of motivation. Participants were making comments like "Why should we teach differently? It doesn't matter what we do if the students won't dig in and work at it. And their parents let them just slide by."

When the problem has been identified in red, switch to the black marker and write, "Under what conditions would I . . . " I asked these participants whether they had ever been disengaged and unmotivated, perhaps in a course or workshop. After various smirks and guffaws, they began to generate some of the items shown in Figure 9.2. After a long silence, one person sighed and said, "We're not so different from the kids, I guess. Those are about lack of skill and peer pressure and how the teacher teaches and what the assignments are like. I guess I need to change."

Investigation of Research and Best Practice

The priorities identified through goal setting should become the focus of staff development efforts during this "Study" stage. In-service days should be devoted to sessions that relate to research and best practice. Requests to attend conferences and workshops should be approved based on their connection to the areas of improvement needed. Study groups could meet to discuss research obtained through sources such as the Educational Resources Information Center (ERIC)[2] and the Educational Research Service (ERS).[3] These databases would be a starting point from which to pursue original studies. Reviews by independent researchers such as Ellis and Fouts's *Research on Educational Innovations* are valuable resources to help evaluate the reports and studies offered by program authors and advocates.[4] School representatives could also be sent to visit sites where exemplary programs are demonstrating progress toward similar goals.

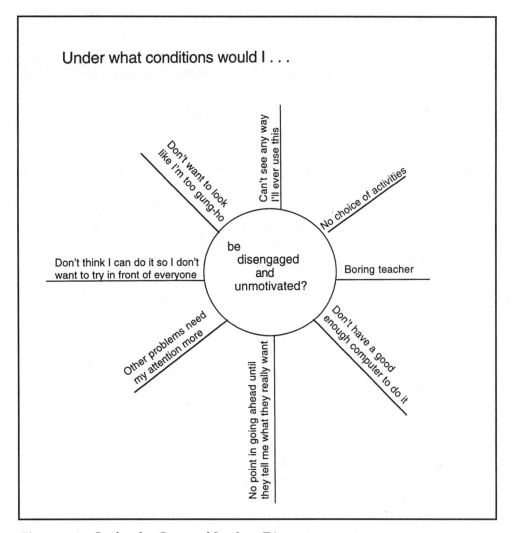

Figure 9.2. Go for the Green of Student Disengagement

The emphasis on data continues during this time of exploration. A study group will have no difficulty finding scores of programs and practices that make marketing claims to boost student achievement and resolve every interpersonal problem in the school. The trick is finding those that can provide data to validate their effectiveness. It's more difficult than you might think.

Kentucky Department of Education officials felt it was important to help school districts identify validated programs, so they contacted about 500 curriculum providers, asking for evidence of their effectiveness. They sought programs that could demonstrate 20% or greater improvement over 2 to 3 years of implementation. Only 64 programs could produce hard evidence, and most contact people indicated that they had never been asked for proof of their results.[5]

The National Diffusion Network conducts a jury process of review before including programs in its *Education Programs That Work* catalog.[6] Just as you shouldn't buy tires that don't fit, don't buy tires without a consumer report.

Evidence of Progress

Figure 1.1 shows an arrow connecting each goal with an "Assessments" box. As we mentioned in Chapter 1 and again in Chapter 8, people need to be engaged in discussions of what evidence would show the goal is being met—not just that the strategies are being implemented. Most of the evidence of goal attainment will be increases or decreases on scores or data already in the school portfolio. Sometimes, especially for goals in the affective domain or for areas we haven't assessed before such as technology applications, new assessments will have to be developed or a process designed for compiling individual teacher observations and record keeping into schoolwide data.

In Chapter 3, we developed a thesaurus of words for assessment so we'd work from a broader definition than paper-and-pencil tests. In Chapter 4, we talked about the important "unmeasurables" that can be defined in terms of observable behaviors. This chapter has been about "studying." The bottom line is that we can use our study time most efficiently if we know what the test of goal attainment is going to be.

Notes

1. Holcomb, E. L. (1996). *Asking the right questions: Tools and techniques for teamwork.* Thousand Oaks, CA: Corwin.

2. The Educational Resources Information Center (ERIC) maintains a database of document and journal article abstracts that can be accessed on-line, on CD-ROM, or through print and microfiche indexes. Call 1-800-LET-ERIC or e-mail acceric@inet.ed.gov.

3. The Educational Research Service (ERS) is an independent, nonprofit firm established by the American Association of School Administrators and other professional associations to serve the research needs of school districts. ERS can be reached at 2000 Clarendon Boulevard, Arlington, VA 22201, by phone at 703-243-2100, by fax at 703-243-8316, or e-mail ERS@access.digex.net.

4. Ellis, A. K., & Fouts, J. T. (1997). *Research on educational innovations* (2nd ed.). Larchmont, NY: Eye on Education.

5. Kentucky Department of Education. (1998). *Results based practices showcase, 1997-98.* Available from the Kentucky Department of Education Bookstore, 500 Mero Street, 19th Floor, Frankfort, KY 40601; phone 502-564-3421.

6. *Educational programs that work: The catalogue of the National Diffusion Network.* (Annual). Funding for the National Diffusion Network has been discontinued. The U.S. Department of Education's Office of Educational Research and Improvement is replacing it with a system of expert panels to identify promising and exemplary educational programs. Their homepage is at http://www.rmcres.com/expertp/index.html.

10

Planning Your Work and Working Your Plan

By this time, you've used data to discover possible needs for improvement, you've used data as one of the criteria to focus on a few high impact goals, you've identified data that will be needed to demonstrate goal attainment, and you've selected strategies that have data to support their effectiveness. Now—as with the new tires on my car—the rubber meets the road. How will the strategies and any new assessments get implemented throughout the school?

Planning

A common characteristic of school improvement "plans-that-never-happen" is that they identify strategies they will use (cooperative learning, a self-esteem program, block scheduling) without analyzing what implementation of those strategies will entail. Any one of the strategies mentioned represents many substeps needed to provide training and support for implementation. When schools select popular options like learning styles and block scheduling, their plans often involve training in the content knowledge without sufficient consideration of changes that need to be made in the school itself to reflect and reinforce those concepts. Although plans will surely be adjusted during implementation, they must be sufficiently developed to clearly represent the magnitude of change they require and the demands they place on people, time, and budgets.

Because an action plan needs to identify specific steps, timelines, and resources, it is important to involve people who have access to information about school calendar, budget, and a "big picture" perspective of all that is occurring in the organization. School teams often find it helpful to include a central office support person in the action-planning stage. If a major innovation such as multiaged classrooms is being implemented, it is advisable to invite a consultant or a team member from another school that is already using the approach. These resource people can provide advice on how they approached the change and even more valuable insights about problems they didn't anticipate and what they might have done to avoid them.

The detail required in action planning often brings the realization that the strategy or approach to be used is a much more complex change than was anticipated. In some situations it is helpful to identify major subtasks and assign a small group to develop that part of the action plan. For example, a major change like multiaged classrooms would need a component of parent education and communication. Involvement of parents in this planning subgroup would be essential.

I've seen school improvement plans in many formats. Some are developed in chart form. Others are written in narrative. Some work well. Some look nice and accomplish nothing. The common elements of those I find useful are specifications of:

- ◆ Steps to be taken and activities that will occur
- ◆ Who will be responsible to guide, coordinate, and monitor the activity
- ◆ Who will be involved
- ◆ Resources needed (money and materials)
- ◆ Time required and schedule
- ◆ Indicators of completion or progress

A simple way to begin is to use these elements as column headings on a large bulletin board or wall (see Figure 10.1). The sequence of planning is "work all the way down, then work across for each activity." In other words, first list all the steps that need to be taken. Because of their training in task analysis, special education teachers are valuable members of the planning group. Repeatedly ask, "And what else will that involve?" This helps the group break down major tasks into their component parts. Also probe by asking, "What would need to happen before that?"

These questions will guide the group to identify missing steps and create a sequence, so the list of steps will need to be reorganized many times. This makes an awfully messy planning chart. It saves a lot of work if you do the first column with stick-on notes. If you write each step or activity on a stick-on note, and then realize you left something out or have things in the wrong order, it is easy to rearrange them.

Activities: Steps to be Taken	Persons Responsible	Persons Involved	Resources Needed	Timeline	Monitoring, Evaluation

Figure 10.1. Action Plan Form

When the sequence of steps or tasks seems complete, have the group work across the chart horizontally for each step. Identify the person responsible for each step and the people who will participate. Discuss whether there is a budgetary consideration. As they move to the timeline column, remind participants that "time is money," too. If released time is needed, there will be substitute costs. If compensation for time outside the contract day must be provided, that cost needs to be estimated. (More about time and money issues later in the chapter.) Timelines should consider the school calendar and capitalize on any staff development days or in-service time to fit with the school's action plan for improvement.

A most neglected but essential column is the last column, often given the heading "Monitoring" or "Evaluation." Too often, this column is simply used to check off completion of the activity. For example, "All staff attended a workshop on cooperative learning." This is inadequate because it does not verify whether anyone actually went back to his or her classroom and applied the knowledge and skills that were learned in the workshop. In Chapter 9, we discussed setting criteria for achievement of the goal. There also need to be indicators that will demonstrate implementation of new strategies by all members of the staff. In Chapter 9, I shared the story of a school leadership team's transformation as the members explored data about absenteeism and created the fish bone chart shown in Figure 9.1. Their decision to create one-on-one relationships for chronic absentees resulted in the action plan shown in Figure 10.2.

Note the careful breakdown of preparation steps that occur before any mentor relationships are established. Also note the specificity of the timeline. Activities are designated by month and sometimes by week. I recently looked at school improvement plans with columns for "Start Date" and "End Date." The plans were already 2 years old when I was asked to review them because the project managers had a sense that nothing was happening. The first thing I noticed was that the timeline columns all had 1996 as start date and 2001 as end date. Given that broad time frame, no one felt much urgency yet in 1997. After all, there were still 4 more years to go. An implementation plan will never move along at exactly its planned pace and sequence. But unless the sequence is outlined, there will be no way to know how far behind we are or what to adjust. The challenge is to strike a proper balance between flexibility and evolutionary planning on the one hand, and patience and perseverance on the other.

Monitoring

Monitoring progress is not always a sophisticated and complicated endeavor. When principals agree to conduct business on the roof or kiss a pig or sit in a dunking booth if students read a million pages—and parent volunteers construct a huge paper thermometer to count the pages read—that is monitoring that can motivate continued effort until the real results (higher reading scores) can be documented.

School: _____ School Year(s) _____

Improvement Objective: To improve student attendance

Members of Team or Task Force: _____

Strategy: Develop 1:1 student-adult mentor relationships for chronic absentees

Rationale: Research findings indicate that student engagement and personal bonding with adults in the school are related to attendance and achievement

Activities: Steps to be Taken	Persons Responsible	Persons Involved	Resources Needed	Timeline	Monitoring, Evaluation
Develop criteria to identify the chronic absentees	Counselors	SIT Subcommittee	Part of June workshop time	During June workshop	Criteria approved by SIT @ August meeting
List the students who need to be involved	Counselor on SIT	Homeroom Teachers	----	During June workshop	Presented & approved by SIT @ August meeting
Set expectations for students who participate	Counselor on SIT	Homeroom Teachers	----	During June workshop	Presented & approved by SIT @ August meeting
Notify parents and get permission to contact students	Counselor	Counseling secretary	----	Before registration in August	Parent permissions returned
Set expectations for adult mentors	SIT subcommittee chair	SIT subcommittee	----	During June workshop	Approval by SIT @ August meeting
Develop training for mentors	Asst. Principal Staff Development Coordinator	SIT subcommittee Homeroom Teachers	Food for picnic	July	Approval by SIT @ August meeting

Figure 10.2. Action Plan—A Completed Example

Activities: Steps to be Taken	Persons Responsible	Persons Involved	Resources Needed	Timeline	Monitoring, Evaluation
Recruit/select mentors	Asst. Principal	Homeroom Teachers	----	July & August	List of mentors
Match students to mentors	Asst. Principal	Counselors	----	July & August	List of possible matches
Hold mentor training and gain commitment	Asst. Principal Staff Development Coordinator	Mentors Homeroom Teachers	Stipends for 2-hour training session ($1200)	August	Mentors sign commitment forms
Hold meeting of students and mentors or make individual contact with students	Counselors Asst. Principal	Students Mentors Homeroom Teachers		August	Students return commitment forms
Determine times & places mentors will contact students	Mentors	Students	----	1st week of school	Schedules turned in to Asst. Principal
Schedule and hold mentor meetings	Asst. Principal	Counselors Mentors Homeroom Teachers	Early release time once per month	Monthly – October through May	Minutes of meetings Summary of student attendance and grades
Re-examine attendance data	Counselors	----	----	Weekly by student; monthly for all	Graph attendance and grades each month as run charts
Plan celebration for mentors and students	Asst. Principal	Students Mentors Families Homeroom Teachers	Budget for food, certificates, etc.	May	Progress certificates to students with % improvement

Figure 10.2 Continued

Take another look at Figure 10.2 and notice the "Monitoring, Evaluation" column as well. You will see two kinds of indicators. They identify evidence that the strategies are being done *and* that the goal is being met. Various documents will be presented and approved, schedules will be turned in, and minutes of meetings will be recorded. This is proof that the plan is being carried out. But the real proof is that attendance and grades will be graphed each month to monitor that the students are at school more and are learning more. This is proof that the goal is being attained.

Many sound, research-based innovations have been initiated in schools, "tried" for a while, and then discarded because "they don't work"—when there has been no way to know whether they have really been "worked." I have already emphasized the need to select strategies that have documented data to back up their claims of improving student performance. But to get the same results, they have to be implemented in the same way in your school. A classic example is cooperative learning. Schools have a one-day workshop for staff on cooperative learning and assume teachers are then ready, willing, and able to apply this powerful approach in their classrooms. A year later, test scores are the same; just as many kids are getting Ds and Fs; and someone in a formal leadership role asks, "Are we doing cooperative learning?" Various people reply, "Oh, sure, I moved my desks into circles." "Well, of course, I do group stuff once a week." Now, I'm not pushing cooperative learning as a magic potion.[1] I am saying that, if you're going to choose a proven program, use it as proven, and prove you are using it—or don't blame the program for your lack of results.

In Chapter 9, I referred to the Kentucky Department of Education's attempt to list curricula and instructional programs that could verify a 20% improvement over 2 to 3 years of implementation. I found it particularly interesting that the introduction to the department's *Results-Based Practices Showcase* stated,

> **Caution!** The most successful practice doesn't just deliver a good program of materials. The personality type of these providers is different than most professional development we have encountered. They are demanding types. They are relatively non-negotiable about performance. They are not timid about asking that a school faculty stop doing what they are used to doing and commit themselves to a new practice. Take note that these providers tend to be much more **demanding about what a school's job is** in taking responsibility for their professional development and ultimate results.[2]

A look at the names of the researchers, authors, and consultants the report describes as demanding makes me feel a lot better about my emphasis on not just "buying the tire," but using it as intended. *Before* all else fails, follow the directions.

Reaping Unexpected Benefits

There's a fringe benefit to monitoring implementation, as one junior high school discovered. Teachers had been concerned about the low self-esteem and disengagement of some students and what they perceived as an overall lack of respect for diversity in the student population. Some of the teachers had been reading about student engagement in learning and a few others had attended a workshop on cooperative learning. They felt that use of cooperative learning might seem more engaging to the students and thereby might increase achievement. Social studies teachers decided to work together and develop cooperative learning activities. Their goal was to have a cooperative learning activity every Thursday and see what would happen.

The data-gathering aspect of their project was overlooked at the time but emerged as an "Ah ha!" for the entire school. After a month or so, the guidance counselor reported at a faculty meeting that for some reason, attendance in seventh and eighth grade was showing an increase and was higher on Thursdays than any other day of the week. He wondered if anyone was doing anything special on Thursdays. When the social studies teachers mentioned their experiment, the language art teachers decided to test it further. They chose Tuesday as a day to use cooperative learning and consciously set out to have the counselor help them trace the attendance patterns. At the time I lost contact with this school, the staff had not yet determined the effects on student test scores, but they had certainly made an impact on student interest and attendance. They had also stimulated the growth of a community of learners in their school.

Finding Time

School improvement, by which we mean increasing student achievement, is neither easy nor cheap. There are important roles for all staff, for a leadership group and task groups, and for a key staff member who works closely with the principal as coordinator and facilitator.

Time for All

This book recommends full engagement of *all* staff at several crucial points:

1. Developing and affirming the school's mission
2. Identifying significant, meaningful data to be compiled for the school portfolio
3. Interpreting the data, requesting more data, and identifying areas of concern
4. Focusing areas of concern to a few priorities and developing goals

5. Participating in study groups to further analyze improvement concerns, select indicators of improvement, and recommend validated strategies

6. Affirming the completed school improvement plan

7. Participating in staff development to learn the use of new strategies and assessments

8. Discussing evidence of progress with implementation and goal attainment

This book provides activities that range in time from 20 minutes to 2 hours. The short activities can be embedded in staff meetings, especially if there is a commitment to devote them to productive professional development activities rather than announcements and housekeeping matters. (One principal used a novel approach to reforming staff meetings and motivating staff to use their new network. He put all announcements and housekeeping matters on e-mail, and if you didn't use it, you just didn't know.)

The longer activities (especially Items 2, 3, 4, 5, and 7) require building some provision such as early release afternoons, late start mornings, or in-service days into the school calendar. One such "window of opportunity" per month is ideal, but staff engagement can occur successfully with one per quarter.

Time for Teams

Unlike many models of site-based management or shared decision making, I stress that a school improvement team does *not* make the decisions about how to improve the school. The decisions the teams make are about how and when to engage peers, students, and constituents in those decision-making processes. Team members prepare, plan, coordinate, orchestrate, and follow up on the work done with the full staff. For this purpose, they need to meet once a month.

The most frequent practice has been to provide substitute teachers so this team could meet during school hours. In some cases, the scarcity of substitutes and the staff members' commitments to their students has led to a different format. In these cases, leadership teams meet for 2 to 3 hours outside the school day and are compensated accordingly. Some schools have been creative in their scheduling, so that planning times of team members are coordinated and meetings can be held during the last hour of the day—partly on school time and partly as additional commitment.

Time for Shared Leadership

One way to symbolize shared leadership is for the principal and a key staff member to cochair the school improvement effort. In this model, the school improvement coordinator is given one less teaching preparation (secondary schools) or is released from supervisory duties (elementary schools) to provide time.

Time Is Money—Finding Money

I'm under no illusions that there's a money tree growing in the arboretum or courtyard of your school. In fact, Wisconsin provides a classic example of school districts facing increased operating costs and salary demands under a legislated revenue cap. Yet, despite this scarcity, I still hear school officials talking about "this money that has to get spent before June 30." And I still get calls in May asking, "What can you coordinate for us in June? We've got some money we could pay some people with." It appears to me that there's money to be had if you have a good plan and also have knowledge of where money comes from outside the district.

The consortium of 16 districts I described in Chapters 2 and 3 has expanded to 28 districts in 1997-1998 and another 10 districts are joining us in 1998-1999. The source of funding for our collaborative school improvement model is Goals 2000. The original application was written to design our process and criteria for participation, and funding has continued as we provide evidence of progress.

In addition to Goals 2000 funding, the Improving America's Schools Act (IASA) provides Title I funding to improve student achievement, Title II (Eisenhower) funding for math and science, Title IV funding for safe and drug-free schools, and Title VI funding for innovative programs. Think about a school improvement plan with two goals: improving student achievement in math and decreasing at-risk behaviors. The first goal fits the mandates of Titles I, II, and VI. The second goal fits the intent of Title IV. The reauthorization of Title I and IASA support the development of consolidated, schoolwide plans. The problem is that most "consolidated" plans are still done as separate projects, just stapled together to be submitted to state departments of education. In a recent meeting, 40 Kentucky educators met to discuss the next steps needed to further strengthen the consolidated planning process in their state. We discussed which aspects of the vision for consolidated planning still have not become reality. Thirty-six of the participants expressed disappointment that there still wasn't evidence of impact on the classroom. Eighteen believed that the biggest barrier consisted of "turf and territory" issues. And 16 noted a lack of broad-based participation at the school and district level. This book has described many ways to get the broad-based participation, but unless people conscientiously *share* knowledge of where money comes from and what it can be used for, schoolwide change will not get the resources necessary for success.

Timing Is Everything

In addition to needing money and time, we need to know the tim*ing* to access the money. Goal setting and planning need to coincide with the budget cycle in the district, so the schools not only know what to ask for but know it before all the money is allocated. Plans also need to be synchronized with the evaluation and application cycles for grant funding as described above.

1997-98 Resources for:
Beyond 2000 - A Continuous Growth Plan
for Educational Excellence

SCHOOL: **MARSHALL MIDDLE SCHOOL**

PRINCIPAL: **Mike Kuehne**
****

Substitute Days = 63 @ $80.75	$5,087.25	Sub
or		or
Stipend Days = 56.5 @ $90.00	$5,087.25	Stipend
Continuous Growth Plan Allocation =	$1,500.00	CGP
Talents Enrichment Allocation =	$1,200.00	TEP
General Staff Development Allocation =	_____	SD
Goals 2000 - Blueprint for Program Improvement =	$1,500.00	G-2000
Collaborative Study Follow Up Resources = (Year) 2002-2003		CS

I.D.E.A. Discretionary Grants:

Middle School Job Shadowing =	$1,500.00	IDEA

Special Education
IEP Writing ($150/EEN Teacher) = $1,425.00   SP. ED.
Title IV - Safe & Drug Free Schools:
      SAP Program = $2,650.00   Title IV

Title II - Eisenhower = $1,200.00   Title II

Carl D. Perkins = $ 300.00   C. Perkins
     SD - Counseling
                        TOTAL: $16,362.25

A plan to spend these resources needs to be submitted to Gary Bersell by October 1, 1997.
See attached form.

{Resource.FmB2000}

Figure 10.3. Resources Available for School Improvement

Figure 10.3 shows how Gary Bersell, Director of Instructional Services in Janesville, Wisconsin, helps principals identify the whole pot of discretionary money that they can tap for school improvement. Substitute or stipend days and Continuous Growth Plan funds were allocated by the district in its budget cycle. The district also filed the overall application for federal grant money and assigned it to sites. The school has until October 1 to finish its plan for use of these funds, and plans must be tied to the school's Continuous Growth Plan.

If your district has never allocated funds in this way before, you may need a fully developed school improvement plan by January—for the following year—so you can be proactive and request these new line items in the district budget. In my experience, schools that make the generic plea, "We can't do school improvement without more money," rarely get new dollars. Schools that have a specific plan for what they will do with the money and how they will ensure it impacts student learning almost always receive some additional support.

Let's imagine that Our Town School identified these goals for its school improvement plan:

1. Students will show improvement in reading and writing skills.

2. Students will demonstrate increased use of conflict resolution strategies and incidents of violent behavior will decrease.

3. All students will apply computer skills in their work in all subjects.

The first goal is an acceptable target for Title I funding, the second goal can be supported through Title IV, and Title II and VI money can be used on the third goal. The school would then need to develop four action plans: one for the reading and writing activities, one for the conflict resolution and violence prevention strategies, one for the family components, and one for the keyboarding emphasis. If the "Resources Needed" column of each action plan (see Figures 10.1 and 10.2) stated dollar amounts and the source of funds from among these grants, *that* would be an example of consolidated planning.

Notes

1. In the (1997) second edition of their *Research on educational innovations*, A. K. Ellis and J. T. Fouts state, "Of all the educational innovations we have reviewed in this book, cooperative learning has the best and largest empirical base" (Larchmont, NY: Eye on Education). Quotation is from p. 173.

2. Kentucky Department of Education. (1998). *Results based practices showcase, 1997-98.* Available from the Kentucky Department of Education Bookstore, 500 Mero Street, 19th Floor, Frankfort, KY 40601; phone 502-564-3421. Quotation is from p. iii.

11

A Design for Data Day

There are at least two schools of thought about visibility and magnitude of change. One is that change should be introduced and occur in small increments to maintain a sense of continuity and not exceed organizational capacity. Another is that people don't get excited about "little" changes, that they don't generate energy and enthusiasm, and that people can hide behind their classroom doors thinking, "This too shall pass." Neither approach is an antidote for natural resistance. In my experience, resistance to the incremental approach may take more passive forms but can be just as detrimental. Introducing change as a major new focus with lots of visibility may generate more overt resistance, but that may be easier to handle when it's out in the open.

I have seen both approaches work when the choice was made intentionally after thorough discussion of the history and current situation of the specific district. The leadership team in East Troy, Wisconsin, chose to build on its past successes and took more of the incremental approach (see "Minimalist Approach" in Chapter 5). The team started its data-driven school-based efforts by providing a timeline of the curriculum and instruction work already done in the district and introduced this new focus as the next logical phase in an ongoing, evolving improvement process.[1]

The school district of Fort Atkinson, Wisconsin, looked at its current situation and saw a number of factors that created a readiness to introduce the use of data as a major new initiative. A new high school building would be opening soon. One round of strategic planning had occurred and a commitment had been made that this cycle would be more data driven than the previous one. The requirements for school accreditation included an increased focus on documenting student success. The year's statewide assessments would be reported in proficiency levels for the first time. All these changes were occurring anyway. Why not capitalize on their common need for data?—especially since participation in a Goals 2000 consortium focused on school improvement provided resources to help answer the "Who's gonna do this and where will we get the time?" questions. Fort Atkinson's decision was to be very direct about accountability issues and engage all 200 teachers in a "kickoff" event. I have helped other districts design "data days," but will use Fort Atkinson as the model for this chapter. Three leaders deserve special acknowledgment: Dr. Jerry McGowan, District Administrator; Dr. Mabel Schumacher, Director of Instruction; and Mr. Joe Overturf, Director of Special Education and Strategic Planning Facilitator.

Purpose

A district might choose a highly visible approach like this for several reasons:

◆ To make everyone aware that using data is an important focus

◆ To convey the expectation that all will support and participate in using data

◆ To ensure that all staff members receive common information about why, what will happen, and how it will affect them

The Fort Atkinson district also had unique local purposes:

◆ To strengthen this cycle of strategic planning with greater use of data

◆ To provide an opportunity for all staff to provide input to the Strategic Planning Team

Preparation

You don't plan an event of this magnitude and visibility just by setting a date and contracting a consultant to "come in and kick off our work with data." I already had some prior understanding of the district because I have worked with some of the local leaders for more than 5 years. Even so, we scheduled an advance day for planning and preparation. Almost 2 weeks before Data Day, I met with a group that included the superintendent, curriculum and instruction staff, all principals, and the facilitator of strategic planning. (The presence and participation of the district administrator in key instructional issues is powerful modeling that I request at all times and reinforce vigorously.)

We began our planning by discussing the purposes of the day. I asked each role group to express what we would need to accomplish for participants to

8:15-8:30	Opening Remarks by Superintendent
8:30-9:00	Aligning School Improvement
9:00-9:30	Why We Need to Use Data More
9:30-10:15	What Data Will We Use?
10:15-10:45	Break
10:45-11:05	Monitoring Our Mission—The First Critical Question
11:05-11:30	The Other Four Questions
11:30-11:45	Swapping Stories
11:45-12:00	What Happens Next
12:00-1:00	Lunch
1:00-1:15	Overview by the Principal
1:15-2:30	Carousel Data Analysis
2:30-2:45	Break
2:45-3:10	Reporting Out
3:10-3:30	Messages for Strategic Planning Team

Figure 11.1. Agenda for Data Day

consider the day a success. This joint list became our set of desired outcomes and our criteria for planning.

After clarifying the purposes, we developed the agenda for a morning session that would include all staff of the district. Since students would not be in attendance, constituents were informed of how the day would be used and were welcome to attend. The morning session was also videotaped so it would be available for anyone interested who could not participate (see Figure 11.1).

We then planned school-based activities for the afternoon so principals could build on the momentum of the general session and staff members could be immediately engaged in authentic work with their own data. Our last task was to develop our respective "To Do" lists in preparation. The handout packet for the morning session included Figure 1.1, the list of data from "The NCA Way" in Chapter 5, and Figure 4.1. We also prepared overhead transparencies of the district and school mission statements. The biggest task—preparing the data that staff members would analyze in their schools in the afternoon—fell to the Office of Curriculum and Instruction. Principals worked on the logistics of the "Carousel Data Analysis," organized the groups, and prepared the reflection questions for each station (see Chapter 7).

District Session

Following a continental breakfast, teachers gathered in an auditorium-style room. I worked from the floor, not from a stage, and used a wireless microphone. These are important considerations, because they gave me the opportunity to move into and through the audience and chat directly with participants. The following sections correspond to segments of the agenda in Figure 11.1.

Opening Remarks by Superintendent

Jerry McGowan opened the session with greetings and humor. His style cannot be captured in text—you had to be there! But he moved quickly from the ridiculous to the reality, describing recent state and local events that generated a sense of urgency for the work of the day: new laws offering public school choice, requests to move in and out of the district, data about the upward trend of home schooling, Youth Options legislation allowing 2 years of technical school after 10th grade, and district comparisons being made in the media and by citizen activist groups. To emphasize these realities, he cut to the quick with dollar figures on revenue lost for each student exercising another alternative and compared these losses with the average cost of a teaching position. He ended on a note of optimism, describing the purposes of the day and asserting his belief that there were data to demonstrate the high quality of the school district and his faith in the staff to help pull it together.

Aligning School Improvement

The second segment focused on the concepts of alignment outlined in Chapter 1 and illustrated on Figure 1.1. To foster active participation, I engaged the group in a musical performance assessment so that I could collect some data to use as an example. Tongue in cheek, I described the controversy about phonics and whole language and the accusations of some citizen groups that students do poorly in reading because they haven't had enough phonics. As a result, I felt I needed to know whether the teaching staff actually knew their phonics and would focus on the long vowel sounds for an experimental test. Their task would be to sing the familiar song, "Row, Row, Row Your Boat," changing position each time they sang or heard a long vowel sound. We would stand for the first "row," sit down on the second "row," stand for the third "row," and continue with our ups and downs for all long vowel sounds (boat, -ly, stream, -ly, -ly, -ly, -ly, life, dream). After reciting the long vowel sounds to activate our prior knowledge and a little humming to practice the tune, we had the administrators model and then we gave it a try. Actually, I gave this group three tries!

I then concluded that, based on multiple observations, about 5% of the group were advanced, 20% were proficient, 55% were at the basic level, and 20% were only minimally proficient. (These were the four proficiency levels introduced with the statewide assessment for the first time that year.) I prolonged the satire by commenting that I was in a district the previous week that had 10% advanced, 30% proficient, 50% basic, and only 10% minimal and by asking them to speculate on reasons why District X was doing so much better.

I used these mock data to bring relevance and humor to a discussion of the alignment between the components in Figure 1.1. First, these data wouldn't mean anything unless we actually cared about whether students could identify long vowel sounds (the content standard) and respond to them by sitting or standing while also singing (the performance standard). If "basic skills" was in the mission statement of Readwell Elementary School and long vowel sounds was one of the essential learnings, these would be important data. It might appear as one of many concerns and surface as a priority learning goal. Then we would study best practice and further analyze our local performance to select strategies.

We might identify the students who were "advanced" and ask how they learned to perform so well. We might even have them tutor the rest of the group. Or we might practice other songs with vowel sounds, have drills of the vowel sounds themselves, or make little kits for more practice at home. Perhaps the music department could help with rhythm, and the physical education department could set up clinics for deep knee bending. We would repeat this same assessment in hopes of better results and might design other forms of assessment to provide alternative demonstrations of the essential learning. Then we would identify who was responsible for carrying out the strategies and administering the assessments and develop our action plans. Spoofing a little kept the large group curious and engaged and still conveyed the concepts of alignment and the big picture of what else happens once data are compiled.

Why We Need to Use Data More

Chapter 2 describes the "Live Motivation Continuum" that was used during the next segment. Audience participation was noisy and energetic. After the applause contest reinforced the factors that would make data meaningful to the participants, I mentioned that "to keep our accreditation" or "to get our Goals 2000 money" were not on the list. They are important considerations but should not be the driving force behind our professional commitments.

What Data Will We Use?

One page of the handout packet included a list of data corresponding to the categories described as "The NCA Way" in Chapter 5. During this segment, I showed examples of graphs from each category and told the story of the school that developed them and how and why. I also showed them the list of data Wisconsin districts must report annually and had them star those items on their handout. This would let them know which data are readily available and also foreshadow the data they would discuss in the afternoon at their sites.

Break

As Figure 11.1 indicates, we worked for 2 hours before taking a break. As a rule of thumb, I try to take short, 10-minute breaks more frequently. But a group size of 200 means longer lines for emptying and refueling, so we needed a long break in the middle. Plan your breaks according to group size and access to personal needs.

Monitoring Our Mission—The First Critical Question

When the teachers assembled at the beginning of the general session, no attempt was made to structure the seating arrangement. Before the break, I asked the participants to raise their hands by building to see where they were and to sit as close as possible to most of the other people from their school after break. Chapter 4 describes the activity we used to answer the question, "What evidence would demonstrate that we are fulfilling the commitments embedded in our mission statement?" Staff members stood and faced each other over the backs of their seats to work in small school-based groups. The transparencies of district and school mission statements were available for review.

The Other Four Questions

Figure 5.1 lists the other four questions for reflection on data selection. During this segment I used the height example to illustrate disaggregation. One petite woman grabbed a chair to stand on, saying she "always wanted to be one of the 6-footers." This was gratifying evidence of the group's comfort level and participation. I encouraged staff members to chat briefly about each question with their neighbors, because in the afternoon they would be asked "what else" they might need to know.

Swapping Stories

The last activity of the morning is described in Chapter 2. By this time, I had spotted some "performers" in the group and recruited them to read the book excerpts.

What Happens Next

We concluded the morning by telling the participants that a "first batch" of data had already been prepared for them to review in the afternoon. We described the process for engagement at their individual schools and emphasized its importance as an opportunity to provide input for strategic planning and to be proactive in determining the data to include in their school's portfolio.

School-Based Activities

Staff met at their respective buildings in the afternoon. Principals prepared for data interpretation by arranging the room, the materials, and the groups as described in Chapter 7.

Overview by the Principal

Each principal created a bridge from the morning to the afternoon by repeating the purposes of the day and using Figure 1.1. The principals pointed out that the afternoon activities related to the "School Portfolio" box and also the column of "Concerns." Participants would review data that would be in the portfolio and identify concerns that might arise from them. They would also identify other data they wanted added to the school portfolio for review before focusing on "Priority Goals."

Carousel Data Analysis

The next segment utilized the process of data interpretation from Chapter 7.

Reporting Out

After completing the round of stations, each small group shared its overall reactions to the complete set of data. Common observations from all groups were highlighted. A list of desired data was also compiled from the sheets at each station. These requests would be forwarded to the Curriculum Office and district staff would help compile as much of it as possible.

Messages for Strategic Planning Team

Each school had a representative who would be participating in the strategic planning process in the next few days. The afternoon discussion concluded by identifying the input this representative should provide from the building.

Follow-Up

The Strategic Planning Team met a few days later. The external consultant was very cooperative and incorporated references to Data Day and the schools' input as the process moved forward. A participant commented that "the information came back and really jelled" in the strategic plan. Joe Overturf, Director of Special Education/Pupil Services and internal facilitator of strategic planning shared with me these helpful comments on the interface between district strategic planning and school improvement:

> This demonstrated how data analysis could be used to complement and enrich our model of strategic planning. It's my belief that information contained within School Portfolios should be used to validate the acknowledgment of weaknesses identified during the internal analysis phase of planning. Currently, sites or districts are asked to develop

a database, but there is not an emphasis on the analysis of the data. In my experiences to date, cited weaknesses are more intuitive on the part of individual planners. I believe that data analysis of pre-existing information would strengthen the basis for identifying critical issues (which is the culmination of the internal and external analysis of the organization).

While data-driven objectives may address the critical issues of the day, they fail to address the objective of dreamers. It's my opinion that if objectives are to be strategic in nature and are to be driven by dreams, then the planning team has a responsibility to identify assessment measures and apply them to those objectives over time to monitor the impact on student learning.

Regardless of the origin of the strategic objectives, i.e., addressing the critical issues of the day or the dreams of the future, there needs to be a conscientious effort to gather data to see if our school improvement efforts via strategic planning are making a difference. I would suggest and hope that some of the information in a School Portfolio be directly aligned with strategic objectives and progress be closely monitored on a periodic basis. This could occur every time there is a periodic review of the site plan. This would provide the vehicle to monitor and demonstrate growth over time to determine if we are having a positive impact on kids.

Other comments on Data Day included these reactions:

◆ It went just perfectly and we are so happy with the level of participation.

◆ This was a wonderful staff development day.

◆ The activities worked so well with that setting of 200 people. It made them all feel involved and even made them laugh.

◆ The morning gave people a sense of purpose and they went away happy to return after lunch and do something that matters.

If you have similar needs and purposes, I don't need a crystal ball to predict that there may be a Data Day in your future.

Note

1. Larsen, S., & Bresler, M. (1998, March). *Involving staff in an evolving process.* Paper presented at the 103rd Annual Meeting of the North Central Association of Colleges and Schools, Chicago.

12

Communicating About Data

They say communication is a two-way street. If only it were really that easy. Communicating about data is more like a traffic pattern of multiple streets, some of which are two-way, some one-way, and some limited to specific kinds of vehicles or special purposes like car pools. Plans for communicating information about student performance must identify multiple audiences, the specific purpose for communication with each audience, and then the appropriate communicators and channels for each audience and purpose. Audiences for communication about data include the media, community groups such as employers and taxpayers' organizations, teachers, students, and parents. The question of who is the appropriate communicat*or* relates to credibility and trust of the audience. Another issue is the vocabulary and background knowledge of each audience. These decisions are further complicated by privacy issues that relate to confidentiality of student information. This chapter provides some general guidelines for communicating about data and describes the approaches taken by two school districts that have successfully built relationships with their communities.

Credibility Begins at Home

I wish I had a dollar for every hour that I had spent trying to help people understand national and international comparisons and find ways to explain to their communities why it's like comparing apples and oranges to compare U.S. test scores with Japan's. We did a pretty decent job of boiling down the concepts into everyday English, but it still came out sounding like a lot of defensive rationalization. And then it dawned on me that most of the folks at home aren't really too worried about international comparisons. It matters a lot to journalists and politicians—but talk to everyday people at the local cafe where breakfast is $2.50 and the regulars have their own tables, and you'll discover they really aren't losing sleep over it. All they really want to know is that *their* kids are doing OK.

Several of these essential ordinary people have pointed that out to me. But I should have known it already. I've been reading the Phi Delta Kappa (PDK)/Gallup Poll of the Public's Attitudes Toward the Public Schools for at least 12 of its 29 annual versions.[1] It was only this past fall, as school districts struggled with "How will we explain that our students look good on national percentiles but not so good on state proficiencies?" that the real implication of one of these findings hit home. Year after year, PDK capitalizes on Gallup's expertise in sampling and surveying to find out what the public thinks. The pollsters repeatedly ask what grade (A, B, C, D, F) the respondents would give to public schools in the nation as a whole, what grade they would give to their local public schools, and what grade they would give to the public school their oldest child attends. In 1997, 22% gave As and Bs to the U.S. national system, 46% gave As and Bs to their local schools, and 64% gave As and Bs to the school their own child was attending. Light bulb! The public in general, and parents in particular, already have more faith in their local schools than in the national system of public education.

This being the case, local school districts would be better off to save the time, energy, and resources they've invested in trying to respond to national and international statistics. The same time, energy, and resources would be better invested in communication that builds on an existing foundation of trust in local schools by local people.

That's why this book emphasizes the use of school-specific data and the involvement of parents and public at the individual school level. Strengthen existing relationships and develop key people as advocates and opinion leaders. At a recent meeting of the consortium of 28 districts I mentioned earlier, participants talked about their efforts to prepare the public for the release of state test data as proficiency levels. Almost every speaker mentioned scheduling community forums—and almost every speaker reported getting all geared up for a mass meeting and virtually no one came. The questions they received were primarily from two groups: the media and a few interested parents who telephoned with specific questions but did not turn out for town meetings. Most parents simply waited until Parent-Teacher Conference night and found out what they wanted to know about their own children that way. Credibility begins at home.

The Birds and the Bees

I remember watching a dear young lady grow up and wondering what she would ask and when and how I should answer. So I picked up a few pamphlets about how to communicate sensitive information to preadolescents. Here is some of the advice I received:

◆ Anticipate what the questions might be.

◆ Be prepared with short, simple answers.

◆ Be as knowledgeable as possible, but don't try to share everything you know.

◆ Answer the questions they ask, but only the questions they ask.

◆ Keep the door open for more questions and more details as they become more comfortable and curious.

I believe this advice applies equally well to informing the public about student achievement results. Of the 28 districts I mentioned, those that received favorable treatment from their local press had met with the writers individually and had not prepared an "opening statement" for their meeting. They simply invited the reporter to come in and asked, "What questions do you have and what information do you want?" They answered, and they gave, and the press was fair.

At the state level, several attempts were made to help districts by developing Assessment Communication Kits and printed materials. The Department of Public Instruction prepared a 16-page "guidette." It didn't reflect the advice above, and it didn't get used by school districts.

On the other hand, the Wisconsin Education Association Council (Wisconsin's largest teacher union) worked with the Wisconsin PTA and developed a single-fold, four-page brochure for parents called *Understanding the New Proficiency Scores.*[2] District administrators and curriculum directors referred to the first two pages (Figure 12.1) as the best resource they had, and it's the publication that got sent home and circulated.

One of our downfalls as educators is that we try to share all that we know instead of figuring out how much our constituents actually want to know. For example, I find myself resenting the weatherman when he tells me I should carry my umbrella tomorrow. I just want him to tell me it might rain. When he takes it upon himself to tell me how I should apply that information, I get downright miffed. Tell them what they want to know, answer their questions—no more, no less.

Offer a Free Test Ride

Of the districts I've worked closely with for the past few years, Janesville, Wisconsin, has the most industry. It's the home of Parker Pen, and General Motors makes cars there. Those companies represent the major employers of the students who *don't* go away to 2- or 4-year colleges. So they judge the school district on the basis of the lowest 30%.

Understanding the New
Proficiency Scores

Parents learn how their children are doing in school in many ways, including teacher conferences, report cards, and graded student work that is brought home.

There is an additional source of valuable information – the scores your child receives on the standardized achievement tests administered each year by the Wisconsin Department of Public Instruction to 4th, 8th, and 10th grade students throughout the state. These tests are called the Wisconsin Student Assessment System Knowledge & Concepts Examinations. As you review the results, keep in mind that test scores are only one indicator of the knowledge and skills possessed by a student, or group of students. Testing experts warn against giving too much weight to the results of a single test because tests measure only a sample of what is taught in school.

The Department of Public Instruction reports student achievement in five content areas: Reading, Mathematics, Science, Social Studies, and Enhanced Language. The scores a student receives in Reading, Mathematics, Science, and Social Studies are based on answers to mostly multiple choice questions, with a few short answer questions. The Enhanced Language score is based on answers to multiple choice questions, short answer questions and the score received on a writing task (an "informative" composition in grades 4 and 8 and a "persuasive" essay in grade 10).

The state tests are called standardized achievement tests because everything, from the directions given to the time allowed to take the tests to scoring and reporting, is made uniform, or "standardized." These procedures ensure scores are as fair and reliable as possible.

What's new this year?

This year, for the first time, two kinds of scores are reported for your child. Norm-referenced scores (such as percentiles) compare your child with students throughout the country. These types of scores have been used in the past.

In addition to norm-referenced scores, this year, proficiency scores also are reported. Achievement for each child is reported in terms of four proficiency categories, or levels. These levels are Advanced, Proficient, Basic, and Minimal Performance.

Figure 12.1. Understanding the New Proficiency Scores

What is a norm-referenced score?

Norm-referenced scores answer the question, "How does my child compare with others?" For example, if your child scored at the 63rd percentile in mathematics, he or she did better than 63% of the students in the comparison group (the national sample) who are in the same grade and who were tested at the same time of year.

What is a proficiency score?

A proficiency score answers the question, "How does the achievement of my child on this test compare with established high expectations for academic success?" A driver's test is an example of a test with two proficiency levels: pass or fail. Whether you pass or fail the test does not depend on how well others drive, but whether you achieve an acceptable level as determined by the driving examiner.

Students receiving a score of Advanced did exceptionally well by showing in-depth understanding of the content area. Likewise, Proficient represents a competent level of achievement. Students who score at the Basic level are achieving at a fairly solid level, although they have some weaknesses that should be addressed. Basic does not mean that your child is failing in the content area.

Children receiving Minimal Performance scores have limited achievement in the content area.

If you are concerned about the achievement of your child in any content area, you should meet with your child's teacher to determine what you as a parent, along with the teacher, can do to help your child do better in school.

The proficiency standards were established in 1997 by parents, educators, and people from business and government at workshops conducted by the Department of Public Instruction.

Why are proficiency scores included in the reports?

Proficiency standards have been established to set high expectations for all students. Comparative (norm-referenced) scores show that Wisconsin's students do better than students throughout the country on nearly all tests. However, a proficiency score judges performance in terms of high academic standards set by people in Wisconsin.

Figure 12.1 Continued

Over the past 2 years, administrators in this school district have made a concerted effort to build relationships with Wisconsin Manufacturers and Commerce. Their mutual goal is to allow teachers, administrators, school board members, parents, and community and business leaders to work together to continue to improve student performance in each local school district.

As part of this effort, the district developed a "WSAS SWAT team." This group guides all information sharing that relates to the Wisconsin Student Assessment System (WSAS). The team includes the superintendent, the district's public relations coordinator, central office directors, and supervisors. The SWAT team identified the following audiences:

- Central office staff
- Principals and assistant principals
- Clerical staff
- Custodial and maintenance staff
- Food service personnel
- CEOs of local companies

Meetings were held for all classifications of district employees, on contract time, to be sure that key messages were heard and understood by all. An official "lesson plan" was developed for all of these meetings. It included explanations of norm-referenced and criterion-referenced tests, district comparisons, and a sample of the kinds of test items students must answer. The messages were:

- Results will look different this year.
- The state of Wisconsin and Janesville schools are expecting more from our students than other states and districts do.
- We will continue to improve.
- We will work together.

"We" was intentionally and overtly defined as district staff, students, parents, community, and the Chamber of Commerce.

For the last audience (CEOs), a special session was planned. These employers were invited to come in and take a "test" ride—that is, sit down in desks with the test booklets and a time limit and "experience the ride." Familiar with high-risk situations, these executives allowed themselves to be videotaped and commented on the nature of the test and their commitment to work with the district. This video was aired repeatedly on the local cable channel. It was a very visual demonstration of the concept of "we." It also illustrates the earlier comment about choosing who the communicators should be. Even if the words are the same, it's a different message when the company president says, "It's a hard test that isn't like the ones we used to take in school."

The Janesville district has addressed one more audience, a group that's most intimately affected by assessment but almost universally overlooked when it comes to communicating the results: **students.** Janesville has two high schools, and the tendency of the media to make comparisons between them has been a concern of teachers and parents. It's a problem that students have tackled this year themselves. Students have written their own article for the media, explaining the test scores and pointing out the absence of any statistically significant difference between the two schools.

Districts in the Big Foot (Wisconsin) Consortium have also involved students through an innovative project in a media class. With a budget of $500 and some clips from a Department of Public Instruction videotape, students produced a documentary about the state assessments that airs repeatedly on their public access channel.

Draw Them a Picture

The school district of Oregon, Wisconsin, is one I hold in high esteem for many reasons. Quality management folks would point to it as an example of constancy of purpose. It has retained the same superintendent for 10 years, a soft-spoken, tough-minded woman who is now president of the state administrators' association. The school district survived the "outcomes wars" without changing terminology or abandoning the effort to clearly identify the cognitive goals it has for its students. It simply took a very heads-up approach to communicating what *we* mean by outcomes-based education *here*, what we are *not* doing, and what we are able to tell you about your children. Moving quickly to data and documentation enabled the district to report percentages of students mastering outcomes, and the accountability the district was willing to provide spoke to the benefits of what it was doing. This history has made the Oregon district better prepared than most for state standards and statewide assessments. It also has made staff members more comfortable using data to demonstrate progress.

It was a new challenge to help parents and the community understand the relationship between national percentile and state proficiency scores. School board members didn't want to hear about testing concepts in the abstract; they wanted to see numbers. So Cal Callaway, Director of Instruction; and Wayne Bellcross, High School Assistant Principal, decided to draw them a picture. Figure 12.2 shows mean national percentile scores—the numbers people are used to—superimposed on stacked bar graphs that show the distribution of students rated as minimal, basic, proficient, and advanced in the new structure. This "double exposure" helps parents and constituents see that their students continue to score just as well as usual compared to the national sample. It also illustrates how dramatically Wisconsin—like other states—has "raised the bar" for student performance.

Students Are an Audience, Too

Much of this chapter deals with the new communication demands that arise from new approaches to assessment, especially state standards and statewide testing. In all of this activity, we must not forget that the first purpose of assessment is to improve student learning—one student at a time. And we must also remember that students hear the news and see the headlines too. On Labor Day, Washington state released the results of the first statewide testing of fourth graders. The day before the start of a new school year, the local paper where our children live ran a banner headline: "FOURTH GRADERS FLUNK." One of those students told me, "I don't want to go to fifth grade because now everyone thinks we're all dumb."

OREGON SCHOOL DISTRICT
PROFICIENCY LEVELS AND NATIONAL PERCENTILES
GRADE 10 -- 1997-98

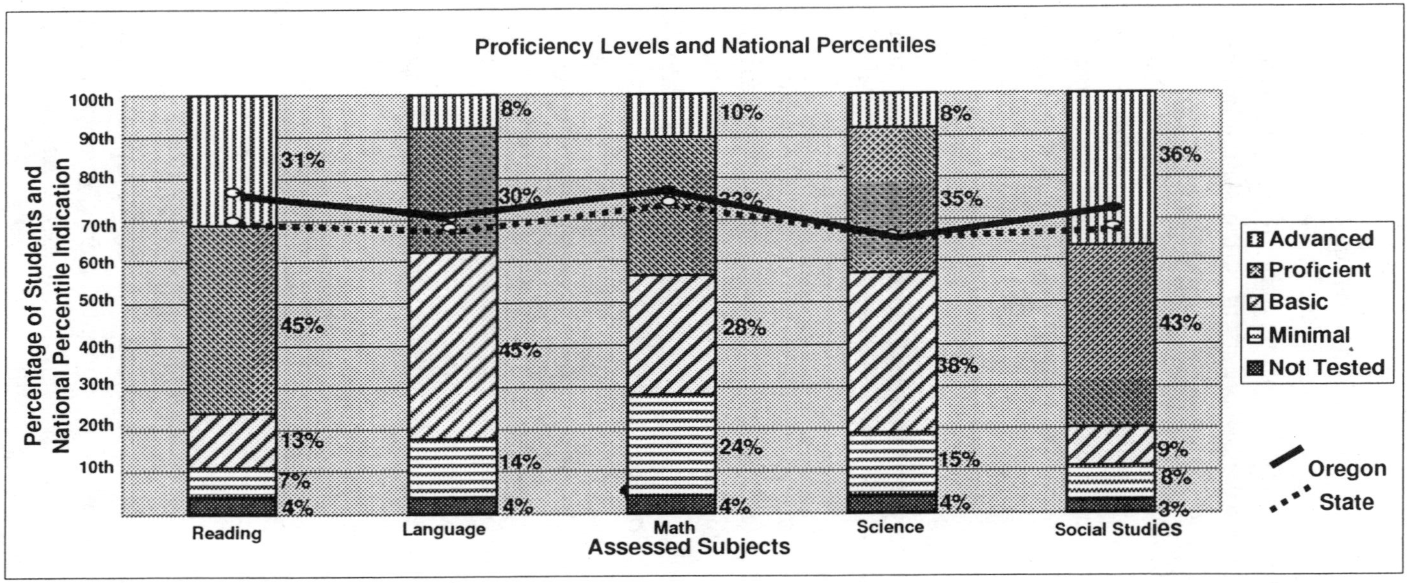

Proficiency Levels and National Percentiles

Subject Areas Assessed	Reading	Language	Math	Science	Social Studies
Not Tested	4%	4%	4%	4%	3%
Minimal	7%	14%	24%	15%	8%
Basic	13%	45%	28%	38%	9%
Proficient	45%	30%	33%	35%	43%
Advanced	31%	8%	10%	8%	36%

WSAS Percentile Ranks			
Grade 10			
	Oregon	Wisconsin	Nation
Reading	76%ile	71%ile	50%ile
Language	71%ile	68%ile	50%ile
Mathematics	76%ile	75%ile	50%ile
Science	66%ile	66%ile	50%ile
Social Studies	73%ile	68%ile	50%ile

*Figures based on students in the school for a full academic year

Figure 12.2. Comparing Proficiency Levels and National Percentiles

Students need to understand that these tests are important, that they need to do their best, but that it's really a check on how their *school* is doing. They also need a clear explanation of what the learning expectations are and a range of opportunities to demonstrate—for themselves as well as for their parents and the public—what they have achieved.

Notes

1. Rose, L. C., Gallup, A. M., & Elam, S. M. (1997). The 29th annual Phi Delta Kappa/Gallup poll of the public's attitudes toward the public schools. *Phi Delta Kappan, 79,* 41-56.

2. Wisconsin Education Association Council and Wisconsin Parent Teacher Association. (1997). *Understanding the new proficiency scores.* N.C.: Authors.

13

Using Student Performance Data to Integrate District Curriculum Work With the School Improvement Process

The focus of this book has been the use of data to align *school* improvement. In Chapter 12, we pointed out that a higher percentage of people believe in the quality of their *own* children's school than the local schools in general, let alone the public schools of the nation. This does not mean that schools exist in isolation. The examples in Chapters 11 and 12 describe supportive relationships between districts and their schools. So how does it all fit together? What about all the emphasis on state standards and assessment? If the school is the focus of attention on student achievement, what happens to K-12 continuity? It's not an either-or question or answer. The district must engage in continuous improvement of the instructional program while every school works to strengthen the learning environment and its delivery of the instructional program.

Going in Circles

Figure 13.1 illustrates relationships between district-level work on the instructional program and school improvement efforts. The three intercon-

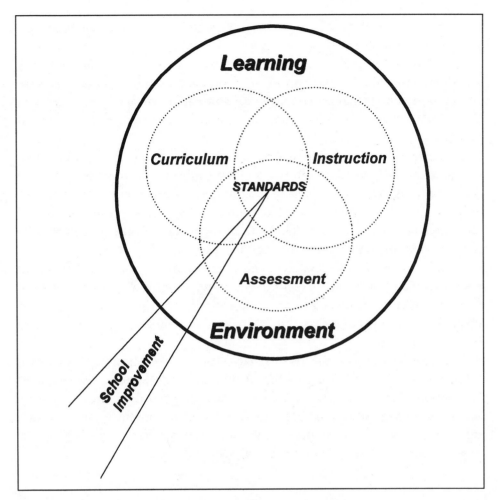

Figure 13.1. Aligning and Improving Student Learning

nected circles represent curriculum, instruction, and assessment. These are the three components of a district instructional program. The overlapping areas of the three circles are referred to as curriculum alignment. The rationale is that students learn more—or at least their scores are better—if there is a tight match between the content identified in curriculum documents, the content that is actually delivered, and the content that is assessed. I have placed standards at the very center, where all three circles overlap, because they are intended to increase student learning by tightening the alignment of the instructional program. We might consider the area marked "Standards" as a magnet, drawing curriculum, assessment, and instruction more closely together.

With regard to these three components of the instructional program, the district has responsibility for determining the curriculum, because the public interest represented through the school board dictates what children should learn. The assessment circle is shared by the district, school, and classroom. Standardized assessments given to all children are selected by the district. Ongoing assessment for diagnosis and feedback to children occurs at the school and classroom level. The state has now become a player in the assessment circle through the increased use of statewide assessments. Instruction refers to the way the curriculum is delivered, and is generally accepted as the domain of the school and its teachers.

In addition to choices about instructional methods and materials, the school is responsible for the learning environment, or school climate. This includes expectations that are conveyed for student performance, how individual differences are recognized and met, and how safety and order are maintained.

The circles of curriculum, instruction, assessment, and the learning environment are like gears that interact and are continuously in motion. Budget considerations may drive a cycle of program review and textbook and materials adoption. External mandates like state standards create a need to look at alignment and perhaps revise the scope and sequence of the curriculum. This is ongoing maintenance of the instructional program.

School improvement cuts across all of the circles. It looks at assessment results and identifies areas of concern where students aren't performing satisfactorily. Then it considers the curriculum and the instructional methods and whether other kinds of assessment are needed to demonstrate what students know and can do.

In automotive terms, the inside circles represent routine maintenance like filling the car with gas, changing the oil, and topping off window washer and transmission fluids. These are done regularly to keep things running well. School improvement is more like what we do when something isn't working right—when we hear a sound we shouldn't, when things groan and grind. These symptoms demand attention, diagnosis, and repair.

Going With the Flow (Chart)

Figure 13.2 provides another look at the relationship between district-level work and school improvement, with data on student performance as the driving force. Boxes with a dark border represent activities at the district level, and rectangles with thinner borders represent aspects of the school improvement process.

The district and the individual schools identify areas of student success and need. For each area of need, the series of questions is asked and answered and plans are made accordingly. Let's use math problem solving as an example. Assuming that students' scores in this area were disappointing, the first question relates to having processes in place to address the need. If there are data to suggest a need to look at math problem solving, it's not appropriate to say, "Well, we'll look at that in 2001, the next time math comes up in the cycle." At the district level, there must be a process or forum in which to address needs as they arise. At the school level, data suggesting a student achievement need should be reflected in the school improvement goals that are set.

Moving on to the "Study" box in Figure 1.1, schools ask questions about the area of student need. Is it in the curriculum? If not, the district's K-12 approach to revising curriculum needs to go into action. Math problem solving

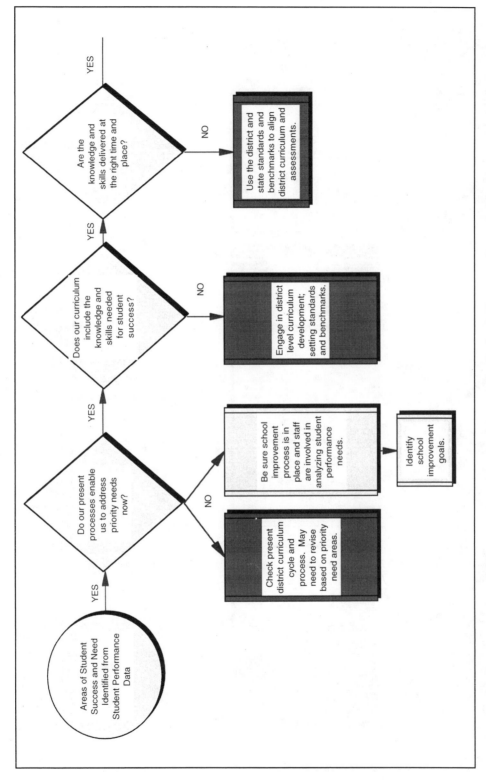

Figure 13.2. Using Student Performance Data to Integrate District Curriculum Work With the School Improvement Process

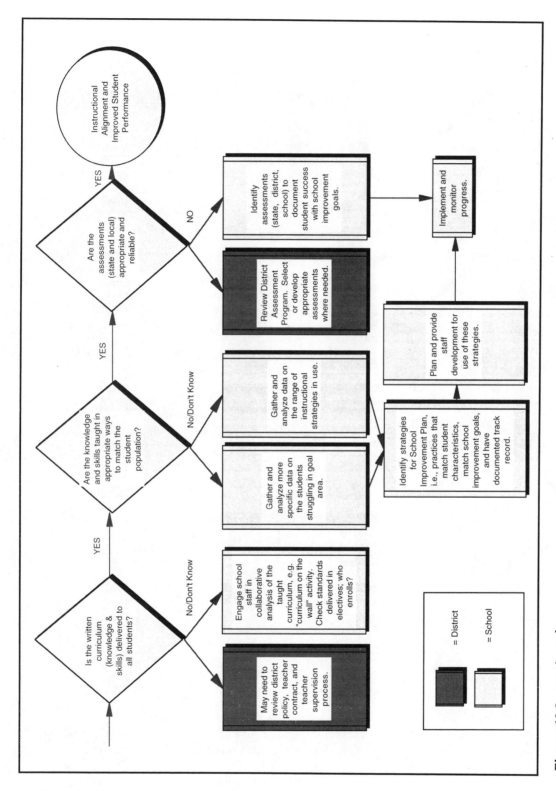

Figure 13.2 continued

may turn out to be in the curriculum but may not be stressed until the next grade level after the major assessment is given. The same district-level process should be used to address needed realignment.

The real problem may be that the written curriculum is not actually being delivered. Most math programs include problem solving as a thread through all units and all grade levels. But it may be a part that's omitted due to time constraints or teacher preferences for computation. The "curriculum on the wall" activity starts with teachers working by grade level to identify the main topics, units, or skills they teach along with time allocations, then cluster them in an affinity process. This may provide a more accurate picture than starting with the written curriculum guides. If it reveals that some teachers are not delivering the curriculum, the district's policies and teacher contracts and supervision procedures should be consulted and utilized.

If math problem solving is in the curriculum and the curriculum is being taught, the next consideration may be the methods that are used and the characteristics of the student population. Further study at the school level would include gathering information on *how* problem solving is taught. Student performance data should be analyzed further to identify the students who are having difficulty and see if they have common characteristics that might provide clues about prior knowledge, learning style, or other barriers to learning that may be present.

School improvement plans would focus on strategies that match the students' needs, address the school improvement goal related to problem solving, and have been proven to increase student achievement of these skills. Once these strategies are selected, the school leadership team develops plans that include staff development so teachers can utilize them effectively. Meanwhile, the district curriculum process is also scrutinizing the assessments that were the source of the student performance data. Their purpose is to analyze the degree to which existing assessments accurately measure the learning expectations and determine the other types of assessment that will be needed to measure all of the expected learnings and provide ongoing information about student progress.

Cycling in Synch

Figures 13.1 and 13.2 are two visual ways of illustrating the relationship between district-level work and school improvement of the instructional program. The circles in Figure 13.1 may provide the best sense of ongoing motion and activity. Figure 1.1 and Figure 13.2 appear more linear, limited as they are by the two dimensions of the printed page. But they repeat themselves in cyclical fashion. In fact, more than one of these cycles may be occurring at the same time, like several sheets of Figure 13.2 intersecting and spinning in a spiral.

The focus is on improving student performance through the mutual efforts of the school and district. As Roland Barth wrote, "When the central office runs a service agency for principals, then principals are able to set up service agencies for teachers, and teachers for children. The chain of command can then become a chain of support."[1]

Note

1. Barth, R. (1990). *Improving schools from within: Teachers, parents and principals can make the difference.* San Francisco: Jossey-Bass.

14

Staying Off the Bandwagons

One of Edgar Allan Poe's famous works is "The Pit and the Pendulum." In my opinion, one of American education's *in*famous characteristics could be titled "The Pits of the Pendulum." Unlike other professions, and unlike education in many other countries, we prematurely embrace change and then impatiently reject it. This phenomenon is variously described as "the pendulum swing," "two steps forward, one step back," and "last year's new thing, this year's new thing, next year's new thing."

Sustaining Focus

A few months ago, a principal told me that "all this talk about data sounds good to the Board but it sure would slow us down." He's probably right, and that would be just fine with me. In Chapter 4, we talked about the need to take time to engage people in discussion of their mission and values and identify data that would be meaningful and useful to them. In Chapter 7, we talked about taking time to involve staff in formulating their own interpretations of that data. In Chapter 9, we stressed the importance of careful study before adopting new programs and practices. In Chapter 10, we emphasized the need to take time for detailed planning of school improvement efforts, so that reference to specific timelines will keep the process moving. We also suggested ways to allocate resources so new efforts aren't abandoned due to lack of support. This chapter makes one final plea to take time about choosing changes, provide time for involvement in the decision making and planning, and stick to those decisions and plans long enough that results can be demonstrated.

Celebrating

"Nothing succeeds like success." I was taught this as one of the precepts of motivating children to tackle new learning. It seems to be equally applicable to adults. We are revived and regenerated when we can see the results of our efforts and know the time and energy we invested paid off. But we can never feel this sense of accomplishment if we don't stick to something long enough to document evidence of the difference it makes. And without some proof, it's pretty tough for even the most dedicated people to sustain the passion that attracted them to work in public education.

If our first problem is that we don't stick to something long enough to verify its impact, our second problem is that we don't plan in advance what that proof would be. This was discussed in Chapter 10. Our third problem is that we forget to "stop and smell the roses." When good things happen throughout the process of change, we don't take time to celebrate.

The April/May 1998 issue of *Tools for Schools*, a publication of the National Staff Development Council, focused on celebration. In an article titled "Applause! Applause! Recognize Actions You Want to See More Often," Joan Richardson described a variety of mini-celebrations—from the "Super Pat" awards given at Adlai Stevenson High School to Golden Plunger Awards and Bungee Cord Awards given for risk-taking, innovative efforts by teachers.[1] This issue includes a checklist for assessing the "celebration quotient" of your school and provides suggested activities and an annotated bibliography of resources about this important aspect of renewing school culture and sustaining focus. If everyone is at the band shell in the park celebrating progress on their current efforts, they won't be standing around on Main Street watching for the next bandwagon to roll into town.

Integrating Programs and Practices

That's not to say there won't be bandwagons. There's always a new trend, a new fad, the hot topic at the convention, the experiment in the next county that we should try, too, so we don't look like we're behind the times. Chapter 9 emphasized the need to absolutely require these advocates to provide proof of their results. And Chapter 10 emphasized the need for specific planning. That doesn't mean a 3-year plan will look exactly the same in Year 2 and Year 3 as it did when it left the drawing board. Better ideas may come along. The strategies that were selected and implemented may not be achieving the desired results. We need to be scanning the horizon all the time to be informed about new developments. But we need to be cautious consumers. The following questions can provide a helpful guide to discussion of whether something new can and should be synthesized with the ongoing efforts of the school or district.

1. *What are the new program's underlying values and beliefs? Do those values and beliefs fit ours?* A lot of programs are packaged with materials and activities that look attractive and appeal to our instincts and intuition. But do they articulate their philosophy? Do they describe the theoretical foundation on which they are based? Is it consistent with the discussions about mission and priorities that have occurred in the school and district? Or, even if it's a good solution for some, will it simply dilute the mixture of energy and effort already under way?

2. *What results does this program promise? Are they the same results that we want to achieve through our goals?* "This is really great for kids," is a claim I hear so often, especially in the exhibit hall at national conventions. Because we care about children, we feel guilty if we don't listen. But how carefully do we listen? In what way is it great for students?

3. *What evidence is there that this program has achieved those results in other schools?* This question was also asked in Chapter 9. When we are trying so hard to produce proof of our effectiveness with students, why do we let consultants and companies off the hook so easily? "It sounds like something kids would like" is an inadequate reason to adopt a new model.

4. *What steps are required to implement this new program? Are there other processes in place in which we do that?* Several years ago, I worked with a group of districts that introduced school-based change and the use of data through the Effective Schools model. Suddenly total quality management (TQM) became the rage and every national association's conference had multiple sessions in a TQM strand. (Some of the sessions sounded suspiciously like something else, with the "q" word woven into the title to gain acceptance.) One administrator who was a cautious consumer attended several and said, "These all seem to focus on teamwork and using data and being oriented to the customer. Isn't that what we are already doing? The last thing I want to do is tell people who are now really committed to our process that we're going to throw it out and start something else!"

5. *What resources are needed to implement this program? Can we afford it?* In Chapter 10, we addressed the reality of resources—not just money but the time and energy of the human resources of the district. Just as individuals can burn themselves out doing good works and end up being unable to help themselves or anyone else, schools and districts can, with all good intents and purposes, exceed their organizational capacity and end up in worse shape than they started. The question of "affording" it is not just a budget question. It's also an issue of commitment, credibility, and constancy of purpose.

Saying No

If a new approach can't answer any of the above questions to your satisfaction, the proper answer is "No, thank you." This can also be true for money. There are times when the best answer to a possible grant is also "No, thank you." If it doesn't match something that's already in your plan and if the time to generate the application and administer the grant and write the necessary evaluation at the end exceeds the benefits it will bring the school or district, you can get along without it just fine. Recently an administrator described a grant opportunity this way: "I was up at 4 a.m. trying to write this proposal when I realized that by the time the proposal was done, I would have put about $10,000 worth of time and energy into the needs assessment for it, and the planning, and all this work—in order to get a $5,000 grant. I threw the stuff away and went back to bed."

Spreading a Little Cheer

In Chapter 3, we talked about using cheers and jeers as a warmup exercise to release tension and energize a group. Even the most passionate people, committed to truth and proof, need celebrations and cheerleaders. Just as change for the sake of change is illogical, crunching data for the sake of spouting statistics is inappropriate. The underlying and overwhelming purpose of this book has been to use data as *tools* to focus our efforts on the real *goal:* maximizing the success of our students. In your study and analysis and planning, in your assessing and monitoring and celebrating, be guided by one teacher's version of a traditional cheer:

Give me a D	D!
Give me an A	A!
Give me a T	T!
Give me an A	A!
Who is it FOR?	KIDS!

Note

1. Richardson, J. (1998, April-May). Applause! Applause! Recognize actions you want to see more often. *Tools for Schools*, pp. 1-2.

CORWIN
PRESS

The Corwin Press logo—a raven striding across an open book—represents the happy union of courage and learning. We are a professional-level publisher of books and journals for K–12 educators, and we are committed to creating and providing resources that embody these qualities. Corwin's motto is "Success for All Learners."